ישיבה תורת חיים

Yeshiva Toras Chaim
Talmudical Seminary/Denver
1400 Quitman Street • P.O. Box 4067
Denver, Colorado 80204
(303) 629-8200

Toras Chaim: Perpetuating our Heritage

The heritage and strength of the Jewish people has always been the precious Torah, which forms the foundation of Jewish life and spirit. The concept of Torah study is not an endeavor limited to any specific moment or location, but rather a primary objective in Jewish living at any time and in any place.

"Study is the life-breath of the Jewish people, the goal of Jewish existence—its purpose and destiny," stated the sainted Rabbi Aaron Kotler, teacher and mentor of the men who head Yeshiva Toras Chaim Talmudical Seminary/Denver. Jewish life stands and falls in the measure of its devotion to study. It is the devotion of scholars which provides the life-blood of Jewish existence even to those limbs which are far removed from the heart. The survival and eternity of Jewish peoplehood depend on the development and growth of scholars. It is they who transmit our spiritual heritage from generation to generation. Without scholars, Jewry lacks the men of wisdom who are the links in the great chain of tradition spanning the ages; and it lacks the educators to instruct the coming generations in the purity and perfection of our eternal tradition.

Yeshiva Toras Chaim Talmudical Seminary/Denver was founded in 1967 on the solid rock of Torah precepts. It was the first Yeshiva high school and college level Hebrew studies program between the Mississippi River and the West Coast. With its foundation firmly entrenched in Torah, Yeshiva Toras Chaim began its upward growth. From that fledgling state, the Yeshiva had grown to a formidable institution.

Over the years, Yeshiva Toras Chaim has demonstrated devotion and commitment—a commitment, not only to the individual development and spiritual growth of each student, but a commitment to transmit our special heritage to Jewish youth, young community leaders, professionals, educators, and businessmen, as well.

Recently, the Yeshiva responded rapidly to an urgent appeal and accepted four young Russian students. The young men came from Moldavia, U.S.S.R. They arrived under a special student exchange program, and the Yeshiva had accepted full educational and financial responsibility for them.

In order to extend its educational horizons, Yeshiva Toras Chaim offers varied Torah learning programs which appeal to many segments of Denver's Jewish community. A wellspring of Torah knowledge is available at the Yeshiva which is unparalleled in Denver. Jewish scholars share their knowledge with those who wish to find their Jewish roots or expand their Jewish intellectual horizons.

Yeshiva Toras Chaim is proud to participate in the publication of this special exclusive edition of Dina Gabel's *Behind the Ice Curtain*, a moving autobiographical account of spiritual heroism during the dark days of the Holocaust. We hope this book will help to increase the awareness of the suffering and plight of the Holocaust victims, and serve as a reminder of the struggle of our people for so many generations. We trust you and your family will find this book a source of Torah inspiration and personal edification.

BEHIND THE
ICE
CURTAIN

———————■———————

ABRIDGED EDITION

DINA GABEL

BEHIND THE
ICE
CURTAIN

■

ABRIDGED EDITION

CIS
P·U·B·L·I·S·H·E·R·S
New York · London · Jerusalem

Published and distributed
in the U.S., Canada and overseas by
C.I.S. Publishers and Distributors
180 Park Avenue, Lakewood, New Jersey 08701
(908) 905-3000 Fax: (908) 367-6666

Distributed in Israel by
C.I.S. International (Israel)
Rechov Mishkalov 18
Har Nof, Jerusalem
Tel: 02-518-935

Distributed in the U.K. and Europe by
C.I.S. International (U.K.)
89 Craven Park Road
London N15 6AH, England
Tel: 81-809-3723

Book and cover design: Deenee Cohen
Typography: Nechamie Miller

Cover illustration reproduced
from original painting by Francis McGinley

ISBN 1-56062-182-6

TABLE OF CONTENTS

PUBLISHER'S NOTE

T HE HOLOCAUST WAS LIKE A GIANT BOULDER HURLED into the pool of Jewish history, the greatest disaster occurring at the point of impact where six million innocent Jewish men, women and children perished in the Nazi concentration camps and ghettoes. But the secondary ripples spread throughout the Jewish community in ever-widening circles, bringing pain, impoverishment, dispersion, exile and despair to untold numbers of Jews across the globe. From the near-victims who just managed to elude the evil grasp of the Nazis to the American Jews who moved heaven and earth to rescue their imperiled brothers and sisters, there was hardly a Jew in the world whose life was not touched to some degree by the overwhelming tragedy of the holocaust.

When the war broke out, the great majority of European

Jews were living in the threatened areas of Poland, Lithuania and the Ukraine, and since the attack came from Germany in the west, the most logical overland route of escape was to the east—into the interior of the vast and exceedingly hostile Soviet domain of Stalin. In the two decades between the Communist revolution in Russia in 1917 and the outbreak of the Second World War in 1939, the professedly egalitarian Communist regime had already shown its true colors. The people of Russia were impoverished and terrorized by the Communist Party, and those that showed any resistance were either executed, imprisoned or shipped off to internal exile in the enormous ice trap known as Siberia.

For the Jews, especially those who clung to their cherished ancestral faith, the repression was particularly brutal as the atheistic Communists strove to obliterate the slightest vestige of religion. But as the Nazi terror advanced from the west, countless thousands of Jews fled eastward into the gaping maw of the lesser evil in the east; if they were jumping into the frying pan, at least they were escaping the fire. Moreover, at the beginning of the war in 1939, when Germany and Russia signed the infamous Ribbentrop-Molotov Non-Aggression Pact dividing hapless Poland between them, the Communists arrested the wealthier people in the Russian-occupied part of Poland and banished their families to Siberia. Thus, by the time Germany violated the pact and attacked Russia in 1941, multitudes of Jewish refugees and deportees were trapped in the Soviet "paradise."

The saga of these Jewish exiles is full of privation and heartbreak. Separated from their families, adrift in a strange and inhospitable land, battling hunger and cold, conscripted into forced labor, constantly in terror of the K.G.B., these people were subjected to the dual trauma of the desperate struggle for survival and the incessant anxiety over the fate of their loved ones who had remained behind and fallen into the grasp of the Germans. But in the end, they were the fortunate ones, because most of them survived the holocaust and participated in the rejuvenation of the Jewish people.

Behind the Ice Curtain, by Dina Gabel, is an intensely illuminating autobiographical memoir which depicts this aspect of the holocaust in great detail and with powerful emotion. It is the story of a young woman from a very aristocratic family in the town of Lida in Eastern Poland, whose father was arrested by the invading Russians in 1939, while she and her mother were deported to Siberia and remained there until the end of the war. Through her eyes, we relive the dismal experiences of both the deportees and the refugees as they struggled to adjust to the harsh new realities of banishment and exile. We feel the numbing pain and grief of separation from home and family. We feel the haunting isolation of being cut off from the rest of the world, like islands in an endless ocean of snow. We feel the degradation of being reduced to living under appallingly squalid conditions and scrabbling for the barest sustenance to keep body and soul together. We feel the devastating anguish and exhaustion of people subjected to backbreaking forced labor from the predawn hours until late at night in arctic cold in the winter and scorching heat in the summer. And we feel the quiet heroism and tenacity of a people who would not allow themselves to be vanquished and their spirits crushed.

The author begins this sweeping book with a very poignant description of her home and family prior to the war, and she adds many more fascinating vignettes as part of her reminiscences while she is hiding from the K.G.B. in a barn in Petropavlovsk. As the narrative unfolds, we discover that the author was the only child of a wealthy and prominent family. In loving brushstrokes, she draws a vivid and touchingly bittersweet portrait of her remarkable father, of his uncompromising devotion to Torah and *mitzvos*; of his vast erudition in Torah and his expansive knowledge and awareness of the world around him; of his close personal relationship with the Chafetz Chaim, Reb Chaim Ozer Grodzinski and many other *rabbanim* and *roshei yeshivah*; of his scrupulous honesty and integrity in his dealings with Jew and gentile alike; of his compassion and numerous charitable endeavors; of his filial devotion to his parents and parents-in-law; of the singular blend of love and discipline with which he brought up his only child; and of the special bond that existed between father and daughter.

The author's memory of her father and her anxiety over his uncertain fate are a constant haunting companion throughout her exile in Siberia, and her aching sense of loss and deprivation springs from the pages with deeply moving power and pathos.

Yet, in spite of her separation from her father, the values he instilled in her were so deeply implanted that she was able to withstand the ordeals of her exile without surrendering her humanity or compromising her ideals. Brought up in the lap of luxury, she was never especially discomfited by the sudden lack of material comforts, only by the degradation and humiliation of being forced to share living quarters with coarse peasants and livestock. Pampered and sheltered as a child, she did not shy away from hard physical exertions and enterprising endeavors to improve the quality of life for her ailing mother and herself. Surrounded by people who abandoned their *Yiddishkeit* in the struggle for survival, she remained steadfast in her devotion to Torah and *mitzvos*, time

14

and time again braving the wrath of the K.G.B. in her refusal to bend or break. In all this, she was supported by her valorous and saintly mother who was a quiet but constant pillar of strength and unquestioning *bitachon*.

In the final analysis, however, *Behind the Ice Curtain* is much more than a profoundly gripping personal memoir. It is an important historical document, a record for posterity of the excruciating experiences of a large segment of the Jewish people during the hellish period of the holocaust, victims of a different sort who persevered and lived to bear aloft again the torch that fell from the hands of their martyred families and neighbors. As such, *Behind the Ice Curtain*, the fourth volume in *The Holocaust Diaries* collection, takes a place of honor beside the distinguished and highly-acclaimed *Late Shadows* by Moshe Holczler, *They Called Me Frau Anna* by Chana Marcus Banet and *Dare to Survive* by Chaim Shlomo Friedman. Cumulatively, these important works—and the subsequent volumes which are presently in various stages of preparation—will provide future generations with an authentic and indestructible testament of the multifaceted disaster of the holocaust and the heroism of those gallant Jews who could be broken in body but not in spirit and will forever stand as immortal champions of the ideals towards which we all must strive.

We feel deeply honored and gratified to have been selected as the publishers of this outstanding book. Our entire editorial staff was deeply impressed by the literary sophistication and extraordinary insight that flowed from the author's talented pen. It was truly a pleasure to work on such a fine manuscript. We would like to take this opportunity to acknowledge the spirited and always cooperative participation of the author in the entire process of bringing her manuscript to publication. We would also like to express our gratitude and appreciation to Michal Steinberger for her invaluable assistance to the author in the preparation of the original manuscript, to Tzipporah Reitman for her painstaking efforts during the editing process, to Editorial Director Raizy Kaufman for her unerring vision and insight in guiding the book through all its revisions to its final form and to the many members of our talented staff whose devoted and conscientious efforts are manifest in this beautiful book. May the *Ribono Shel Olam* look upon our labors with favor and grant us the privilege of continuing this work to bring glory to His Name and inspiration to His people.

Y.Y.R.
Lakewood, NJ
Adar 5752 (1992)

BEHIND THE
ICE
CURTAIN

—————————■—————————

ABRIDGED EDITION

PREFACE

HEN MY GRANDCHILDREN CAME TO YERUSHALAYIM during their vacation in the summer of 1986, shortly after the tragic death of my husband, *zichrono livrachah*, I told them a few stories about the war years, which I spent in Russia. They were fascinated; they wanted to know everything about the war and about what life was like before it. When their vacation was over and it was time to return to New York, they made me promise to write down whatever I remembered.

It was almost a year before I was able to begin. I did not have any references other than my own memory, but I do, *baruch Hashem*, remember a great deal. I have always kept the memories alive; the good years I wanted to remember, the bad I couldn't forget. My memoir is not a thriller but a day-to-day account of the hard times and good times, and I tried to present both as accurately as I could.

As paragraph after paragraph began to flow from my pen onto the pages of my notebook, I realized it might be a story not only for my grandchildren but also for their peers, parents and others as well. Besides my personal experiences and reminiscences about my family and forebears, it touches on the most horrible period in the history of our people, and of many other nations as well, a tragic period which spans more than seventy years.

Two experiments were undertaken in our "enlightened" twentieth century—not with laboratory mice and guinea pigs, but with human beings, with people. The first experiment was the Communist Revolution, the attempt to create a theoretical utopia which violated all rules of nature, even from the secular point of view. In the process, its executors emerged as the most brutal and inhuman tyrants, forswearing and stifling all vestiges of belief and religion; scruples and morality were thrown to the winds. The Communist Revolution aroused the lowest instincts in the pursuers of power, and in the pursuit of this power, millions were killed and oceans of blood spilled.

The second experiment was undertaken by the Germans. Their goal was to rid the world of Jews. The outcome is only too well-known. In the resulting holocaust, six million Jews were murdered and burned.

These two experiments have many things in common. For the Jewish people, the most significant common factor is the price we paid in blood. The Germans, with their Teutonic efficiency and "scientific" methods, managed to murder six million Jews in five years, while it took the Soviets seven decades to achieve almost the identical results. In addition to the hundreds of thousands, possibly millions, of Jews who were shot and tortured to death in the Russian prisons, how many more Jews were lost through spiritual annihilation! Is a spiritual holocaust less of a tragedy? In times past, if a Jewish son or a daughter converted or married out of faith, the parents would observe the traditional *shivah* mourning period for the child, who was henceforth considered dead by the parents and lost as Jews. Thus, by attempting to destroy the Jewish faith, the Soviets were in effect destroying untold numbers of our Jewish people. I consider the Communist holocaust, in its full scope, no less grave and devastating than the Nazi holocaust.

The Jewish people are veterans of tragedy. After the destruction of the holy *Beis Hamikdash* by the Romans and our subsequent dispersion throughout the world, the Spanish Inquisition stood out for centuries as one of the bleakest tragedies in our history. But although the Inquisition took many thousands of lives, the Jews at least had the option of leaving the country and continuing to live as Jews. In the experiments of the present century, however, there were no such options. The German experiment culminated in near total physical annihilation, while the Soviet experiment enchained the Jews behind an iron curtain, with the slightest attempt at observance and adherence to our religion resulting in imprisonment and torture in the gulags or in death.

For a Jew in the Soviet Union, particularly during the three decades of Stalin's rule, it took superhuman courage, will power and endurance, often at the risk of losing his life, to keep *mitzvos* and observe the commandments of our Torah. Still, there were some Jews who, regardless of all danger, clung to their principles and beliefs, unsung heroes whose stories have yet to be told. Among the new books dealing with this era is the heartbreaking and heartwarming *Deep in the Russian Night* by Rav Aharon Chazan, which was recently released by C.I.S. Publishers, who are also the publishers of this book.

At this point, I would like to express my deep respect and recognition to C.I.S. Publishers for undertaking the publication of *The Holocaust Diaries*. It is a most worthy and important project documenting the personal experiences of survivors of the holocaust from the Torah point of view, people whose faith in the Almighty bolstered their spirits and kept them beyond the reach of their tormentors and persecutors. I am also very pleased and honored to have my memoir included in this distinguished collection.

I would also like to acknowledge my deep and sincere appreciation to Rabbi Yaakov Yosef Reinman, Rabbi Alexander Zissel Ellinson and Mrs. Raizy Kaufman of C.I.S. Publishers for their warm attitude, thorough insight, personal involvement and cooperation during the entire process of preparing my book for publication. Working with them was a very rewarding experience.

I am also grateful to Michal Steinberger of Yerushalayim, for her integrity, skill and intelligence in helping me coordinate my original manuscript. Special thanks are due to my good friends Reine Hochster and Fay Tanzer for their constant, enthusiastic encouragement.

But my deepest thanks go to my children and grandchildren on whose request I started to write the book and whose love and invaluable support brought it to fruition.

I offer up my most heartfelt and profound thanks and prayers of gratitude to the *Ribono Shel Olam* for granting me the *zchus* of seeing my grandchildren grow up in an atmosphere of Torah values, *chessed* and ethics, which their parents instilled in them since their earliest years. Their *midos tovos*, *yiras shamayim* and strict adherence to *mitzvos* surpass even my grandmother's wishes for her own children. And I pray to Him that the luminous light of the holy Torah shall always shine upon them and upon all the generations to come.

CHAPTER 1

■

Our Fate Is Sealed

WOJNA! WOJNA! WOJNA! WAR! WAR! WAR! THIS ONE word repeated three times set the world on fire. The words were pronounced, after a long silence, on Polish radio at five o'clock in the morning on Friday, September 1, 1939.

Ten days earlier, large posters plastered on every available surface had announced the general mobilization of all Polish military forces, and from that moment on, a choking uneasiness, a cold shiver, a feeling of predestined doom had overwhelmed us. There was no escape now. We felt as if we were locked in a small cubicle with a sagging ceiling liable to collapse at any moment and bury us beneath it.

Hitler had made no secret of his plans; long before the outbreak of war, his craving for blood and *Lebensraum* (expanded living space for the German people) had been distinctly spelled out in his book *Mein Kampf* and his fiery speeches. Nor did he bother to conceal his specific objectives, which included, among many others, to exterminate the Jewish race, to establish the dominance of the "pure" German race, to eradicate the forces of Communism and to recapture the Polish Corridor. The League of Nations had awarded Poland this narrow strip of land after the First World War to allow it access to the Baltic Sea, thus cutting off part of Germany from the rest of the country. Every time a German wanted to travel from Berlin to Koeningsburg, he had to have his documents checked by Polish customs officials, and to the Germans, more than any other people, this was particularly galling.

Those few kilometers of land gave Hitler a convenient pretext to start on his quest to fulfill his broader goals, to conquer Europe, demolish Russia and rule the world. When it became clear that war was imminent, we knew that Poland, the geographical stepping-stone to Russia, would not be spared.

For a number of years before the war, the Germans had carried out their slogan "armaments instead of butter" to the letter, raising taxes and stockpiling arms. Poland would be the first target, a small nation to consume on the way to Russia. This was expected. What was not expected was the sudden rapprochement between the two demons Hitler and Stalin, when their respective foreign ministers Ribbentrop and Molotov shook hands and signed their infamous non-aggression pact.

Poland, crushed and in flames, ceased to exist sixteen days after the outbreak of war. Hitler satisfied himself temporarily with western Poland, while Stalin marched unopposed into eastern Poland after two weeks of German bombardment. For the Germans, it was a small price to pay for Russian non-interference in the German campaign to conquer western and northern Europe.

Though the farthest Polish town from Germany, my hometown of Lida was one of the first to be bombed. At seven o'clock in the morning, two hours after the outbreak of war, sirens were already screaming and airplanes roaring overhead. Explosions were heard from several directions.

We had a very good shortwave radio, and a few days earlier, while spinning the dial, I had accidentally intercepted an order given in German, "The first three cities to be bombed are Cracow, Gdynia and Lida."

Cracow had been the historic capital of Poland from medieval times until Poland was dismembered in 1793 by the imperial predators Russia, Austria and Prussia (the forerunner of modern Germany). When Poland regained independence at the close of the First World War in 1918, the capital was moved to Warsaw. Nevertheless, Cracow retained prime strategic importance because of its close proximity to Austria and the military bases and airfields in its vicinity.

Gdynia was the only Polish port on the Baltic Sea, located at the tip of the Polish Corridor, that narrow strip of land which divided Germany into two parts.

Lida, close to the Russian border, had two military regiments stationed there, one infantry and one air force. It had a big airfield, an air force pilot training school, hangars and airplane repair shops. In addition, Lida was an industrial center. Among other things, there was a big rubber factory, which had been leased by the Polish government for the last six months before the war and dedicated exclusively to the production of gas masks.

The military bases around our town suffered heavy damage during the German bombardment, much of the destruction due to sabotage by the numerous German spies who infested Poland. One such case of sabotage took us all by surprise. It involved a certain Polish air force captain who was in charge of ordering brass parts for the airplanes from my father and Uncle Yaakov. The airplane repair shops were our occasional customers, and this captain was their purchasing agent. I distinctly remember the inflated pride and aloofness, characteristic of most Poles, with which he used to enter our office. His manner was unfailingly rude and impertinent.

On the second day of the bombing, Saturday, September 2, 1939, three German airplanes were shot down by Polish anti-aircraft guns after the airbase in Lida was already in flames, and the body of the very same Polish captain was found in one of the downed German planes. It was no wonder that the Germans had known the exact locations of their targets.

On September 17, 1939, Russian troops, preceded by hundreds of armored trucks, tanks and all kinds of military hardware entered our town. In the beginning, many townspeople greeted them with a sense of relief that Lida would at least avoid German occupation. In the sixteen-day war, the center of the town itself hadn't been damaged at all. The main bombing was directed at the outlying military bases and the industrial area, in which we lived. Fortunately, although the bases were destroyed, not one bomb in the industrial area hit its target. The beneficiaries of this good fortune, however, were not us but the Soviets.

Shortly after they took possession of our territory, the Soviet system was put into effect. The nightmare of Stalin's regime soon started to show its true face. Stores were emptied, and long lines, extending out to the sidewalks, Soviet style, materialized wherever anything of value was still available. Among the shoppers were many Soviet military men and their wives, who were astonished to find hundreds of stores filled with all kinds of merchandise in a small town such as ours. "Just for presents," they used to say to rationalize their sharklike appetites. Even after the stores were emptied, the owners were ordered to keep them open, and since no new goods became available, they were accused of hoarding. Many storekeepers were indeed guilty of "stealing" their own goods from their own stores and selling them secretly for black market prices.

The N.K.V.D. (National Commissariat [Ministry] for Interior Affairs) and K.G.B. (Commissariat for Government Security) became involved. Why bother buying when confiscating was easier? As a result, a horde of commissars appeared on the scene, assisted by members of the underground Polish Communist Party, who had been imprisoned under the old democratic Polish government.

When the Soviets opened the prison doors for them, the Polish Communists had felt like heroes and partners to the holy cause, but they didn't enjoy their freedom for long. After a very short while, they were arrested by their Soviet liberators and charged with treason. "If you were real Communists," the accusation went, "why didn't you overthrow your government?" I had the opportunity to meet some of these erstwhile Polish Communists in Siberia, after the amnesty for Polish prisoners who had survived. Their idealism had long since evaporated, and their new and only goal was to reach the free world.

I remember the visit of the first two commissars who came to our factory. One claimed to be some kind of technical expert. The other was in charge of the financial side of the proposed deal. They were polite, courteous and urbane, obviously having been instructed to act that way. They asked to see the owner and the plant.

The factory was still in full operation, by order of the Commissariat and in accordance with typical Soviet waste, using up raw materials and confiscating the products of industry. My father and the main engineer showed the commissars around, explaining every detail of the operation. The commissars gave the impression of clients interested in purchasing the plant. After they finished their inspection of the plant, they went back into the office and started their inspection there.

Our office consisted of three rooms on the ground floor of a new four-story building. The first was a big room, its width divided by a long counter. Behind the counter was a row of desks, wall shelves, file cabinets and, in a corner, the steel vault. In front of the counter, at the far end, were two doors. One door led to the office shared by my father and Uncle Yaakov. The other led to the office shared by my cousin Doctor Simcha Eiges and the head accountant.

At that time, I was working in the office, and I was there when the commissars and my father returned from their inspection of the plant. As they began their inspection of the office, the "financial expert" took over. He didn't even bother to examine the books. Instead, he asked for the keys to the vault and the combination to open it. In the vault, we kept notes, stocks, policies, cash and personal items, such as my mother's and my aunt's jewelry and family heirlooms. The commissar took out every item, made a detailed list, put everything back, folded the list and put it in his pocket.

"Not a thing may be taken from the safe," he said,

courteous but firm. We knew what he meant.

The commissars also went into the other two rooms of the office and gave the same order. "Everything must be left in place."

There was also another door off the main entrance, and passing through, the two commissars encountered a large room with rows of benches. On the far wall stood a narrow cabinet with a fringed velvet curtain. In front of it, on a raised platform, was a pulpit, also covered with a fringed velvet cover.

"What is this?" they asked with an expression of bewilderment. "What do you do in this room?"

"It is a *molelnia*," answered my father. "A synagogue."

"A synagogue in a factory?" They burst out laughing.

With an air of skepticism, the commissars started a thorough inspection of the room. They raised the curtain on the *aron kodesh*, removed the cover of the *bimah*, opened the drawers and checked the shelves, but all they found were *siddurim* and other *sefarim*.

After the inspection at the factory, they invited themselves to the house. Since it was dinnertime anyway, I went along. As we entered the house, the maid was setting the table, and we had no choice but to ask them to join us for dinner. During the meal, the commissars played the role of charming guests, complimenting the food, discussing various subjects and admiring our perfect Russian accents. Despite her profound sense of foreboding, my mother played the part of the gracious hostess and participated in the conversation as calmly and intelligently as she did with more pleasant, genuine guests.

The Russians' behavior surprised us. We knew we were dealing with the devil incarnate, so why the pretense? It was surely intended to confuse us, to make us less cautious, as if to say, "You see, we are human. We'll not do you any harm." But when they finally left, we weren't all that confused. Rather, we were deeply worried. We sensed what was going to happen.

That same evening, my father and my uncle took the *Sefer Torah* from the *shul* in the factory to one of the *shuls* in town for safekeeping. Fortunately, the commissars had not put it on their list.

Two days later, six commissars arrived, our two "experts" and four others in N.K.V.D. uniforms. There were no more smiles now, but masks of gray stone and harsh words like sharp knives.

"According to the order of..."—and there followed a long litany of paragraphs and articles—"the Government of the Soviet Union is confiscating the plant, the house and all of their contents."

They gave us two weeks to vacate the apartments, ours and my uncle's, and only allowed us to take our personal belongings. Our fate was sealed.

CHAPTER 2

■

Confiscation and Arrest

I T WAS STILL POSSIBLE TO RUN, IF ONE WAS WILLING TO take a risk. But our family was so close-knit that one brother wouldn't leave without the other, nor one sister without the other. To make matters more complicated, Uncle Shmuel, a younger brother, had fled the Germans just a few weeks before and came to us with his wife, two children and his wife's parents, both eighty-seven years old. There was no other choice but to remain in Lida.

On the day we moved out of the house, two long lines of Polish and Jewish workers positioned themselves in protest at the gate.

"We will not let our bosses leave!" they yelled. "We want them here. They are like brothers to us!"

The workers blocked the way but were removed by force.

Three of them were arrested on the spot. What a spectacle this was for the Russians! Employees defending their blood-sucking employers? Unheard of! Finally, as a concession to the workers, the new bosses appointed my cousin Mendel, Uncle Yaakov's son, as manager of the plant, but fearing that an arrest would inevitably follow, Mendel escaped the next day to Vilna and from there to Kovno. Unfortunately, two years later, he shared the fate of most Kovno Jews at the hands of the Nazis.

After the Russians occupied eastern Poland, a contingent of Russian troops entered sovereign Lithuania as well. To mollify the Lithuanians for this invasion, they allowed Lithuania, which still had nominal independence, to annex the famous city of Vilna, known as "the Jerusalem of Lithuania." In medieval times, Vilna had belonged to the Grand Duchy of Lithuania, as had Lida, Novogrodek and other towns in this part of northeastern Europe. In the fourteenth century, Lithuania had been joined to Poland following the marriage of Prince Jagiello of Lithuania and Queen Jadwiga of Poland, and at the end of the eighteenth century, after the dismemberment of Poland, it had come into the possession of Czarist Russia. After the First World War, when Lithuania, Latvia, Estonia and Poland had regained independence, Vilna and the neighboring towns became part of Poland. Kovno now became the capital of Lithuania, but Lithuania never gave up her claim to Vilna. And now that the Russians had allowed Lithuania to take back Vilna, it became the natural destination for many thousands of Jews who were fleeing the Germans.

The only road to Vilna from western Poland passed through our town of Lida, which was only ninety kilometers away. And so, tens of thousands of Jewish refugees streamed through Lida on their way to Vilna. While Lida had originally been home to thirty thousand inhabitants, its population swelled to one hundred thousand or more during the period of the exodus. Countless Jewish refugees spent a few nights in Lida, sleeping in private homes, *shuls*, schools, even the streets, as they waited for the opportunity to cross the border. Many Lida residents also joined the exodus. At first, the Russians were lenient about border crossings, but after a while, they clamped down and many refugees were arrested.

The housing situation in Lida became desperate. Besides the thousands of refugees who needed a place during their brief stay in town, the Soviets had also requisitioned many apartments for themselves. Entire families were squeezed into one room, with the rest of the house occupied by the Soviet officials and their families, who had come along in the belief that Hitler would keep his word and the Soviet occupation would be permanent. The richer and more prominent families were put out of their homes altogether. Indeed, the lower a family's social standing, the less it suffered. And so, when we were ordered to move, it was next to impossible to find another apartment.

It took my father and uncle most of the two-week grace period before they came up with a "find" at the other end of town behind the tiny, cramped house of Rav Mordechai Shmuckler, one of the *roshei yeshivah* in town. It had two small rooms with a tiny kitchen, conveniences in the back yard and an entrance straight from the outside, which meant that the wind, rain and snow blew right into the middle of the tiny kitchen every time anyone opened the door. The outside was not even a street but a vegetable garden. Without enough space for his own large family, Rav Shmuckler had nonetheless offered us the little hut he had at the other end of his garden. It looked like, and probably had been, a gardener's hut. With the same grace and dignity my mother had exhibited while running our big and elegant house, she now cooked the one-pot meals in the tiny, cramped kitchen.

My Uncle Shmuel and his family had better fortune. Having fled their town Suvalki a few days before the war started, right after the announcement of the general mobilization, my uncle had been able to bring a large part of the merchandise of his huge textile business and some of his furniture, which he deposited in one of our warehouses. He found a four-room apartment, as well as a big storefront with back rooms into which he transferred his merchandise just before the Soviets entered our town. Half a dozen of his salespeople, who had fled together with him, joined by another half a dozen locally-hired people, worked until exhaustion measuring, cutting and selling, liquidating as much of the inventory as possible before it would be confiscated.

Our machinery, though, stopped selling as soon as the war started. Wholesale business, our main line, died completely, since many of our customers were from abroad. In Europe, they were from Romania, Latvia and Lithuania, in South America, from Brazil and Argentina, where small agricultural establishments were using motorless machines like ours. In Poland itself, there was absolutely no interest in our products. Food, shoes and clothing were sought after, not ploughs, threshers or straw-cutters. And since such items couldn't be hidden or carried away under an overcoat, we were left with literally nothing at all when our factory was confiscated.

By the time we had to move, Uncle Yaakov's children, his son Mendel and daughter Sonia, with her husband Simchah and their small child, had already fled to Vilna. (Simchah's father was the well-known *rav* Reb Henoch Eiges of Vilna. He was one of the *gedolei hador* and was considered the leading authority on divorce law.) As my parents and my uncle and aunt were inseparable, it left the five of us to fit into the new flat. There was barely enough room to stand or sit. One of us had to go to Uncle Shmuel's apartment every night to sleep. As we were allowed to take only our personal things, we weren't crowded by furniture, pictures, carpets, lamps or any of the other items which had surrounded me since my childhood and were so dear to me. But even our personal things needed much more space than the two tiny rooms could provide. We took some things to Uncle Shmuel, a valise or a carton went to one friend or another, and so our few remaining possessions found their places in several locations around town.

The packing was a very sad ordeal. Most of it was done by my father, myself and my father's two sisters on a visit from Grodno. My mother was always spared any physical strain. Being perfectly organized and orderly, she was only given the task of deciding which of the more valuable things had to be packed separately.

The thriving business in my uncle's "textile emporium" didn't last long. The confiscation order reached him when only a small part of his huge stock had been sold, but it still left him with a sizeable amount of Russian currency, *chervoncy*, which was pretty solid at the time.

Sharing was the rule in my father's family. If Uncle Shmuel had money, a part of it would naturally be given to his two older brothers. My father's two sisters Yocheved and Esther also received equal shares. They lived with their families in the town of Grodno, also occupied by the Soviets.

Though they were well off before the war, after the occupation they suffered the same misfortune we did.

When my father's two sisters came to visit from Grodno, it was a very sad reunion, indeed. How different from the joyous family reunions we had shared just a short while before! Was it just a nightmare, a bad dream? Was it possible that in the span of only three months our world could collapse?

We sat huddled, hands clasped in our laps, avoiding each other's eyes, unable to find words to say to each other. It wasn't only the material loss, it was the loss of our entire lives' work in every field, our striving, achieving and hoping. We felt suspended in the air, uprooted, afraid to think about tomorrow, about the next moment. The confiscations and evictions had come too suddenly, not giving us time for our new status to sink in. But under the Soviets, things can always get worse. Just when you think you've reached the bottom of a pit, you suddenly realize there is another, even deeper one into which they are ready, mercilessly, to throw you.

With an aching heart, I looked at my father. How worried and forlorn he was now. My dear father! How I adored him! I knew he wasn't worried about himself. He was concerned for my mother and me and the rest of the family. I also knew that, considering our uncertain future, he was particularly worried about me, his only child, since at the time I was twenty-two years old and not yet married. He was always so courageous, so energetic, so capable of handling any situation. Always full of hope and *bitachon*, a pillar of strength for the rest of the family.

My father's righteousness, his honesty, his love for people, his *midos tovos*, his good deeds, his ability to get along with people from all walks of life, were all unmatched. He was liked, admired and respected by all who knew him or knew of him, except the N.K.V.D. For them, he was too prominent, too good a person. They had a special place for people such as my father. And so, my father was the first of the group of capitalists that had to be removed.

One winter afternoon, on January 7, 1940, three N.K.V.D. men carrying rifles with fixed bayonets entered our dwelling. A truck was waiting outside. They produced a document, and after reading the all too familiar, horrible paragraphs, they called in two other soldiers who had been waiting on the truck. Just as hired movers would do, they started carrying valises, cartons and trunks which were piled up in one of the two rooms. There had been no place to unpack them, and now they were being taken away. We stood motionless, as if hypnotized, and watched.

When they finished, one of them turned a page he was holding in his hand and called out, "Which of you is Eber? You'll come with us," he said. It was my father.

As if in a trance, my father took his overcoat and started moving toward the door.

Then one of them said, in a fit of humanity, or maybe sadism, "Say good-bye to your family, because you'll never see them again."

My mother fainted, my aunt ran to help her, my uncle froze. My father turned, but I knew he didn't see us. His eyes were overflowing with terror and tears.

I started to cry hysterically, "My father, my father! He is an angel. He hasn't hurt a fly in his life. All he ever did was help people. Why are you taking him?"

"If you don't stop, we'll arrest you, too," the N.K.V.D. men said.

I clung to my father's arm and reached out to kiss him, but

at that moment, he was brutally pushed out the door.

Sobbing bitterly, unaware of the fierce cold, I ran outside. There was another car behind the truck, the N.K.V.D.'s windowless "Black Maria." I saw how two of them pushed my father inside, climbed in behind him and slammed the door.

And so the door was shut on my father's meaningful and fruitful past, on his promising and hopeful future. It was slammed on all those happy years I had had the *zchus* and privilege to live and benefit from the wisdom, warmth and goodness of my father's unique personality, from the ethics he had taught me, not only with words but with deeds and examples. Would I truly never see him again?

CHAPTER 3

■

Like Wilted Leaves

NO MATTER HOW HARD I STRAIN MY MEMORY, I HAVE NO recollection of how and when I went back into the house and what happened during the rest of the day. I do remember seeing a dim, foggy, bluish-gray rectangle of the night sky through a window. I stared at it for a long time.

I looked at my mother. In the semi-darkness, I could see that her eyes were open, looking at the ceiling. She lay next to me, fully dressed as I was, quiet, not moving, not crying. To my left, I saw Aunt Gittel, sitting next to us in a chair.

"Yaakov," my aunt said quietly to her husband. "Go lie down for a while. Your staying up all night will not help anyone."

My uncle didn't answer but continued swaying and looking at the window, which was becoming gradually brighter, announcing the birth of a new day. Finally, slowly, he turned from the window, unable to face the new day. He went to a little cabinet and took out his *tallis* and *tefillin*. He held them in his hands, as if not knowing what to do next, his mind far from the confines of the room.

"D-D-Dina," he said to me, stammering slightly as he always did when distraught or nervous. "G-go at once to Uncle Shmuel and warn him not to come to us. It is dangerous to be seen visiting the family of an arrested person."

I looked again at my mother. With such a heavy stone in my heart, I couldn't imagine how I could stand up or walk out of the house, but I felt I had to obey my uncle. My mother nodded, barely moving her lips. "Go," she whispered. I went.

The winter of 1940 was the coldest in memory. Temperatures reached thirty-eight to forty degrees below zero Celsius. People used to say that the Russians had replaced the shortage of food, fuel and other goods with Siberian cold.

It was a fifteen-minute walk from our place to Uncle Shmuel's. During the night, a fresh blanket of snow had covered everything in sight. A frozen fog obscured the way. Not a soul was on the street; it was too early for people to start the day. When I arrived at my uncle's house, they already knew. A former employee of ours, a devoted friend, had been on his way to visit us and, from a distance, had seen what was happening and rushed to my uncle to warn him. From the looks on their faces, I could tell they had spent the night the way we had. My Aunt Etie, always neat and elegantly dressed whatever the time of day, was disheveled and shivering, terrified that the N.K.V.D. would come and take her husband, too.

They didn't know the details and were sure that Uncle Yaakov had been arrested together with my father. Hearing that Uncle Yaakov had been spared gave them some relief. As it was Thursday, my aunt insisted that we should not prepare anything but spend *Shabbos* with them instead.

We arrived on Friday afternoon, shortly before *Shabbos*. My Uncle Shmuel and his two sons Shulem and Dodi had beautiful voices, but this *Shabbos* the *zemiros* were recited quietly. We spoke little. Our thoughts were with my father. Where was he now? In prison or still held at the N.K.V.D. headquarters for interrogation?

During *Shabbos*, I forced myself to suppress my feelings, but the minute *Shabbos* was over the whole weight of agonizing pain I had felt the day before returned with full force. My father! My father! How could you be taken from us? Dear, dear father, how you must be suffering at the hands of those bloodthirsty monsters! I knew then that unless I would see my father again, the searing pain in my heart would not diminish for many years.

The day after my father's arrest, waves of panic engulfed our town. My father had been arrested because he was a wealthy businessman, an "exploiter of the workers," and every person of means or position understood that his arrest would not be an isolated incident. Regardless of the tightly closed border and the severe cold, a frantic exodus took place. People went to smaller villages around Lida and hired peasants who took them by sled to the Lithuanian border and then on foot to the other side. Some were caught and arrested, some were lucky and escaped. Mostly, it was the young and the men who took the risk. Their families stayed behind, assuming that the Russians wouldn't harm women and children. They hoped that after the war, somehow, the men would rejoin them. Many others remained in town, thinking, in the way of human nature, "It happened to someone else. Maybe I'll be spared." Some were, many were not.

The N.K.V.D.'s Black Marias became a familiar sight now. They abandoned the practice of working only at night and were rolling through the streets twenty-four hours a day. When the "upper class" was weeded out, the "liberators" started their harvest in the ranks of the many "isms" with which our town abounded. Right, left and in-between—it made no difference.

After my father's arrest, we stopped having any relationship with the people of the town. Besides my Uncle Shmuel's family, no one would visit us, nor would we visit any but our closest friends. Meeting people in the street was a painful experience, for even family friends and those whom I knew well would turn away when they saw me or even cross to the other side. On occasion, if we met at a friend's house, they would excuse themselves and mutter their apologies. I understood their motives; they were afraid. Clearly, it was as painful for them as it was for me.

Although the Jews under the Polish government were considered second-class citizens, they could still expect a certain measure of justice. In cases involving the government, there was at least a possibility of presenting evidence, calling witnesses and so on. Soviet justice was something else altogether. The whole world had had a glimpse of it not very long before the war, in the infamous prefabricated Moscow Trials of 1936-1937, when Stalin's hatchet sent the heads of his own kin rolling into the gutter. The execution of hundreds of thousands before and after the trial should have taught us something, but it didn't. We still couldn't believe that the Soviets, whom we saw walking, talking and looking like humans, might not be human. It was our mistake.

After a long deliberation with my two uncles, it was decided that I should see a lawyer. It was also decided that my two uncles should remain in the shadows. My mother was too heartbroken and sick now to be able to undertake any action, so it was up to me to act on my father's behalf.

In our business, we had never used a lawyer. If once or twice a dispute with a customer or a dealer did occur, it was settled between the two sides without any further complications. My father and Uncle Yaakov would come rushing into the house, open the *sefarim shrank* and take out the *Shulchan Aruch* (the Code of Jewish Law). Though they were both scholars well-versed in all the details of the laws, they would check the relevant passages meticulously again and again for only one purpose–that the other party should not be mistreated. With gentiles they were even more careful not to cause *chillul Hashem*. Contracts, when needed, were drawn up as simple agreements, without any confusing small print.

Nevertheless, I knew many lawyers in Lida, some of them personal friends of my father. I spoke to them. They were honest enough to admit that they were afraid to get involved in such uncertain circumstances. Their, or any, intervention might do more harm than good. They were right. Only one lawyer suggested that I write to Stalin himself, addressing the letter to the Supreme Soviet in Moscow, to describe the details of my father's arrest and plead for his release.

I wrote a long, heartbreaking letter, but it was as ludicrous as saying "please" when you ask a hyena to stop sinking its teeth deep into your neck. The sleepless nights, worry, sorrow and fear destroyed our ability to think clearly. Had I really believed that my letter would go further than the N.K.V.D. in Lida? Evidently, it did not reach Moscow but wound up instead in the hands of the prosecutor in Lida. A few days later, I was summoned to his office.

The moment I stepped into the waiting room, I had an unpleasant surprise. It was an insignificant incident, but my tension and fright magnified it to disturbing proportions. The receptionist was a girl I knew well, though we weren't exactly good friends. Her parents were well-to-do people whom I also knew well, and I had never suspected her of having Communist connections to the extent that she should become the prosecutor's receptionist. I suppressed my surprise and said a friendly "good morning." She didn't answer. How quickly she had learned their tactics! Her face was cold and hard, and only her big gray eyes smiled a triumphant smile, without shame, showing delight in my agony.

She looked at the list on her desk and in a loud voice asked, "What is your name?"

I didn't answer her question. I just said that I had come to see the prosecutor. She made a mark on the list and turned to the next person.

When my turn came to enter the prosecutor's office, a ton of lead welded my feet to the floor. I felt the room spinning as I walked through the door. I faced a short, bald man, with a red, round face and slits for eyes. I remember only a few fragments of his words: "You are an enemy of the Soviet regime . . . will be sent away . . . no letters should be expected . . . go now to the N.K.V.D. department." I was in a daze. The bright daylight looked black. I had incurred the wrath of the Soviets, and now, the threat of exile like a heavy weight suspended by a hair. My letter had been a big mistake. It had placed me in jeopardy, and perhaps my father as well.

I remember standing in a big room, my eyes glued to a little silver purse in the shape of two clam shells. It was lying on the floor together with many other pieces of silver that had belonged to us, like a pile of wilted leaves swept into a corner of a garden. Awareness returned to me. There were a few N.K.V.D. men in the room. Two boxes of *sefarim* were standing near the door. One of the men threw a small bundle on top of one box. I was still looking at the purse. Like a child pleading for a toy, I kept repeating, "This little purse was a present from my grandmother. Please give it to me." I couldn't tear my eyes away from it, as if everything we had lost was contained in that little purse.

"Sign the paper, take your boxes and your bundle and go," the man said, ignoring my pleas for the purse. On the paper was written that everything they had taken when arresting my father had been returned to us. They had taken almost everything, but I signed anyway. What else could I have done?

I found a man with a cart who took the two boxes with the *sefarim* to Uncle Shmuel. In the bundle were two tablecloths. Everything else they had taken—silver, furs, clothes, linen, utensils—they kept. We had to manage with the few daily items they had left around the house. Still, we were happy they hadn't burned the *sefarim*. At least that profanity was spared.

The days that followed were hard to bear. Many of the other prisoners were allowed to write letters and to receive packages, but my father was kept incommunicado. The thought that my letter might have been the cause of my father's harsh treatment constantly gnawed at my mind. For now, we knew he was still in the prison in Lida, but for how long? None of the arrested men was expected to be spared slave labor in Siberia, or worse. Families who communicated with the prisoners and knew the destinations to which they would be deported might have a chance of being reunited if there should ever be an amnesty. But they had told my father to say good-bye forever, so perhaps his fate had been sealed from the start.

The pain was unbearable. For four months, my father was imprisoned in Lida. Hundreds more joined him. Every second Monday morning, the families were allowed to bring a parcel, which was checked thoroughly by the guards before being taken to the prisoners. In the fierce, bitter cold, a long line of women, or sometimes a man or a boy, each holding a bundle, waited for the gate to be opened. Only three or four at a time were allowed in. There was no talking in this line, only desperate, worried looks and sighs. I knew many of the people. Often, a woman lamenting loudly, another swaying and dissolving in tears, would leave the gate carrying the bundle she had brought. "The name was not on the list," they would say. "Who knows what happened? Was he sent away or taken to a punishment cell?" Without the food we brought, the warm winter clothing, the blankets, how were the men to survive the treatment in there? But unfortunately, my bundles were never accepted.

The prison was halfway between our apartment and Uncle Shmuel's, on the Third of May Street. Every second Monday, after waiting for hours at the prison gate, instead of going home, I would go to Uncle Shmuel's house, leave the parcel in the hall and collapse on the couch and cry until I was out of breath. How could I tell my mother or Uncle Yaakov? Shmuel was younger, healthier and not as attached to my father as Yaakov was. Only two times out of eight had the prison officials selected one small item and returned the rest, a sliver of butter from a bar, a few pieces of toast. But even this was a consolation. My father wasn't entirely forsaken.

Then one Monday, at the beginning of April, 1940, the

guard didn't open the gate. He just waved us away, saying, "Don't come any more. The prisoners were taken to another place."

How much suffering can a person endure? We were soon to find out. I never paid much attention to dreams, but one I had on April 11, just before daybreak, was different. It seemed like a telepathic message.

In my dream, I opened a door and saw a very large, completely empty room. I went inside. At the same moment, I saw my father entering through another door at the other end of the room. We were slowly moving towards each other and reaching the center of the room. I noticed a thin white net spread from wall to wall, dividing the room in two. Simultaneously, we stopped on either side of the net. My father, clad in white, didn't smile or speak. He only looked at me, raised his index finger and wrote the number "13" in the air. The room dissolved in a fog, and I woke up.

The dream seemed uncannily real, and it disturbed me deeply. I felt sure that it carried a terrible message, but I could not be sure what that message was. The authenticity of the dream was confirmed to me much later, when people who had been with my father in prison told me that his cell number had been 13. Clearly, my father had given me a sign that he was trying to communicate with me and that the dream was not just a figment of my tormented imagination.

I didn't mention the dream to anybody. It was too painful for me to speak about my father. The wound was open and bleeding.

CHAPTER 4

■

In the Dead of Night

ON FRIDAY, APRIL 13, A FREEZING COLD DAY TOWARDS the end of the interminable winter of 1940, I made one of my regular visits to Uncle Shmuel's and Aunt Etie's apartment to spend the night. It was a few days before *Pesach*, and I remember being very tired. I slept on the couch in the dining room. As it was Friday night and there were no maids to turn out the light, a single bulb was left burning all *Shabbos*. Thoroughly exhausted, I fell asleep immediately, grateful for the comfortable couch and unaware of the burning bulb.

Suddenly, I was rudely awakened. What was it? A thunderbolt? An earthquake? I tried to open my eyes, but a sharp beam of light was blinding me. A man was tearing at my arm and shining a flashlight in my face. I heard my Aunt Etie's sobbing voice, "Dina, Dina."

"*Vstavay! Vstavay!*" the man ordered. "Get up!"

He took the flashlight away from my face, but pulled my arm again.

"*Vstavay!* "

There were three of them, carrying rifles with fixed bayonets.

Again, I was forced to listen to a long document with endless paragraphs. Toward the end, I heard the words, "And therefore, you are considered an undesirable and hostile element, and you have to be deported to a distant region of the Soviet Union."

"My mother," I cried. "Where is my mother?"

"Get up. We have no time. You'll see your mother later."

I looked at my wristwatch. It was one o'clock in the morning. They had come for me in the dead of night. I heard Uncle Shmuel's voice in the foyer. My hands were shaking, my teeth chattering, and my stomach was convulsed with cramps.

"Quick, quick, let me go to the bathroom," I pleaded.

"Where is it?" they asked.

"It's outside, on the backstairs landing."

Two of them followed me. One stood near the top of the staircase, the other held the toilet door handle.

"*Skorey, skorey,*" I heard his voice, deliberately low-pitched so the neighbors shouldn't hear us. "Hurry up. It's late. Your time is up."

I went back into the apartment. Aunt Etie stood near an open suitcase throwing in clothing, shoes, whatever she could get her hands on. Uncle Shmuel was running from room to room, wanting to help but only getting in the way. Then he emerged with a toothbrush in his hand.

"Dina, don't forget this," he called agitatedly.

The stony-faced N.K.V.D. man laughed. "You'd better give her a loaf of bread," he said. "She'll need it more than the toothbrush."

Even in my half-crazed state, I saw the ironic truth in his words.

In the meantime, Aunt Etie was packing another valise, then a bag. One of the N.K.V.D. men ordered my uncle to take the valises downstairs quickly. My uncle tried, but they were too heavy. He tried again, and he dropped them on the floor again. Perhaps the fear had drained his strength. Impatiently, one of the N.K.V.D. men grabbed the valises and rushed out the door. My aunt threw a coat on my shoulders and put a bag in each of my hands. With a rifle-bearing N.K.V.D. man on each side, I went down the flight of stairs to the street.

I was aware of everything, but I felt as if I were seeing it from another planet, that I was split into two separate selves. Outside, an open truck was waiting. I saw people, bundles, valises, all thrown together in one pile. It was still dark, and I couldn't figure out how many people there were on the truck. No one was talking, but children whimpered and were hushed by their mothers. I turned to take a last look at the house. Two dark silhouettes, reflected in the half-moon, were standing inside the entrance and crying. I wondered why I didn't cry myself.

The truck began to move, but after a few minutes, we came to a stop. There were noises, and another heap of human cargo was loaded on top of us. Then it was straight to the railroad station. As we neared it, we were joined by more and more trucks. It seemed that the N.K.V.D. had been very busy that particular night. The trucks reached the station, but they didn't go to the passenger entrance. Instead, they continued on and stopped about a hundred meters from the building.

People, bundles and children started dropping from the trucks like rubble in a demolition. Women were crying, and children were screaming uncontrollably. We were divided into groups, then we were herded with barks and roars to the station platform. There we saw a long line of heaps of bundles and people, spaced at even distances from each other. From afar, they looked like heaps of stones along a newly-built road. Dragging ourselves and pushing our luggage, hustled by guards and sentries, each group fell into a separate heap.

The night, as if ashamed, now let the day take over, and a pale orange glow appeared on the horizon. Children were still crying. Women were tripping, falling, losing their bundles. Soldiers' boots were pounding the concrete platform, their ankle-length army coats flapping in the air, one hand holding the rifle straps, the other holding big white sheets of paper. Names were called and checked. Finally, when we were told to stop in front of a huddled, shivering group of people, surrounded by their haphazardly packed and hurriedly gathered worldly goods, my heart leaped. I saw my mother sitting on a bundle.

My mother didn't see me. It was cold, and she had pulled her woolen cap low over her forehead. Maybe she had closed her eyes, not wanting to see the pandemonium around her. I touched her shoulder.

"Mama, I'm here," I said.

She looked up with an expression of bottomless sadness, which gradually changed into a faint, ethereal smile. It barely touched her lips and disappeared, and then she started to cry hot, heavy, silent tears.

My mother seldom cried and never complained. She wasn't strong physically, but she had an iron will and control. Her stamina and endurance, her rock-hard belief that every move a person makes, everything that happens to him, good or bad, is willed by the Almighty, sustained me more than my youth and health many times in the years to come.

"I told them where you were," she said quietly. "I gave them the address. I didn't know what to say."

"Mama, it was the only right thing to do," I comforted her. "I would have come to join you anyway. Do you think I would have stayed behind if you were taken away? At least, we'll be together."

"They came to us at eleven-thirty and gave me fifteen minutes. I didn't have anything in which to pack. Aunt Gittel made two bundles. This one I'm sitting on has the pillows and quilts. The other one, wrapped in the yellow bedspread, contains our clothing."

My mother kept her hand on the yellow bundle, and while she spoke, she unconsciously dug her fingers into it and tightened her fist, as if wanting to be sure she still had these last few possessions.

A scene flashed through my mind. It had not been so long ago, only about five or six months before the war. It was late afternoon, but there was still bright daylight. My father and a guest were sitting in the dining room drinking tea and engaging in an intense Talmudic discussion. A little notebook bound in black patent leather was lying on the table near my father. The guest was a *mashgiach* in a well-known *yeshivah*. He was one of the many *roshei yeshivah* and *mashgichim* who used to visit us regularly, always leaving with a sizeable contribution. A moment of silence interrupted the discussion. My father sighed.

52

"Mr. Shapiro, why are you sighing?" the *mashgiach* asked. "Look through the window. As far as the eye can see, all these are your properties. What do you have to sigh about?"

My father put his hand on the little black notebook, patted it and said, "These are my possessions. All that you see through the window—none of that is really mine. Only this I can call my own." And he again patted the little book. It contained the entries of all his donations. A prophetic vision! How truly it came to be fulfilled, just a few months later. All his possessions were confiscated, but the *zchus* of his *tzeddakah* and *chessed* could never be taken from him.

A sharp whistle from a locomotive brought me back to reality. Hissing and clanking, spitting smoke and steam, the engine, pulling a long chain of red cattle cars, slowed down and stopped at the other end of the platform. A fresh commotion erupted. Guards rushed about in all directions. Shouted orders crisscrossed each other in the early morning stillness. Wide, screeching doors opened to reveal dark, empty interiors, like the jaws of giant beasts ready to swallow the heaps of people sitting in front of them.

There were two guards in front of each car.

"Take your things and get into the wagons!" they bellowed at us.

I looked at the people around me. There were only women and children. I didn't know any of them. They were all Poles whom I had never met. Near other cars, I saw familiar faces, but there was no time to say a word. Jews, Poles, White Russians, we were all in the same boat. We hoisted our bundles into the cars and climbed in after them. The guards closed the doors and erased our past.

By this time, it was already six o'clock in the morning. Outside, a new day was being born. Inside, there was only a timeless darkness. The few rays of light coming through the tiny windows didn't reach the floor. We trampled on the bundles and on each other's feet, bumping and tripping in the dense gloom. Slowly, our eyes adjusted to the darkness. We recognized our things and sorted them out. In the absence of bunks in the cattle cars, each family, or rather half-family, piled up its bundles against a portion of a wall to serve as seats and beds. Ours was the space nearest the door and under one of the four small windows. There wasn't enough space to spread out, and we realized we'd have to sleep sitting, if sleep would ever come.

My mother and I noticed we were the only Jews. *Pesach* was a few days away, and my mother suddenly realized she had forgotten to ask Uncle Yaakov for *matzos* to take along. Somehow, he had been able to get them for all of us, but in the rush of leaving, she had altogether forgotten about food, let alone *matzos* and so had Aunt Gittel. I checked the bags Aunt Etie had put in my hands. Thankfully, they contained food. A *challah*, a cooked chicken, their whole *Shabbos* meal. She had given it all to us. At the bottom, I found a bag of sugar, a cup, even plates and forks. The other bag was bulky but light. It was her pillowcase, tied in a knot. Inside there were *matzos*!

"Oh, Mama!" I exclaimed. "We have *matzos*!" We couldn't believe our good fortune.

One thing that Aunt Gittel had remembered was my mother's *siddur*, but we only found it later when we reached our destination. For the meantime, we were too disoriented to collect our thoughts to *daven*.

A sudden sharp jolt pulled our train forward, then backward, then a turn to the left and it stopped. I climbed on top of our valises, and looked out the tiny window. We had only moved to a farther track, the fifth from the platform, according to my count. A few minutes later, a passenger train pulled into the station, blocking it from view. I turned away from the window. We were cut off, excluded from the outside world.

Time was passing. We were locked and bolted into our communal isolation. There were about forty people, including children, in the car. Judging from their appearance and dress, they represented a very diverse group. However, one woman, with an infant in her arms and a three-year-old, was noticeably different. She was unwashed and in rags, with an expressionless face, bulging eyes and saliva dripping from her mouth. She looked feeble-minded, as did her little girl. All her possessions consisted of one bundle, wrapped in a dirty, homespun cloth and a pail. From all sides, glances started to turn in the direction of the pail. Since there were no sanitary facilities, we saw in it our salvation.

"Yes, you can use it," she said with a lisp, visibly appreciating the attention she was getting.

We couldn't understand why such a person should be deported. She told us she came from a small farm village, that her husband was a farm hand, but even in such an obscure place, politics took their toll. Some time before the war, elections had been held for a *soltys* (village representative) in her village. Two candidates competed, both had supporters, and the elections ended in a tie. A fist-fight resulted, and each side spited the other by electing this woman's husband to be the *soltys*. He could barely sign his name, but when the Soviet authorities took over, they still saw in him a "potential threat" to the regime and arrested him. And so, this poor woman joined the other deported families of arrested husbands. She was taken from bed three days after giving birth. Listening to her story I felt consoled; there was somebody worse off than I.

The day outside brightened and lent a bit more light to our wagon. The children, after crying all night, were asleep now. I counted the people. There were thirty-three adults and six children, the oldest a boy of about six. My mother and I had a neighbor only on our left side; to our right was the door, which couldn't be blocked, so we were not so cramped. We sat on the bundles just as we had on the station platform the night before. My mother leaned against my shoulder and dozed off. I saw the fatigue on her face. I kept my eyes open, unable to sleep. All the emotion, even the exhaustion, was gone. I felt a complete emptiness.

Many of the women opened bags and took out food. In one hand they held a piece of bread, in the other, a chunk of meat or cheese. I categorized them by the way they ate. One tore ravenously at the chunk she had in her hand, both cheeks bulging, stuffing in another bite before swallowing the previous one. Others held their food daintily with their fingers, took small bites and chewed slowly. I didn't understand how they could eat.

My mother, as if reading my mind, said, "Dina, it is *Shabbos* today. We are not supposed to fast. But first we must wash our hands and say *berachos*, at least. Will they bring some water?"

I looked at my mother in admiration. At such a time, to think so clearly! I knew it was *Shabbos*. We had just had a *seudah* last night, a lifetime ago. But to think of *Shabbos*? Of *mitzvos*? With my whole life just torn out from under me, I couldn't think past the bundle at my feet.

It was almost noontime. We waited. Another hour passed. We heard trains coming, trains leaving. I heard some sounds outside our car. Someone was fumbling with the lock and the bolt. With a shake and a push, the door was flung open. The guard put his head in the wide opening and, impersonally, as if talking to a vacuum, announced, "Today you'll receive only water. Bread will be delivered tomorrow."

A sigh of relief fluttered through the air. Water! How precious it became when it was lacking! Soon, the other guard deposited two pails of water on the floor near the door. How smart of Etie to have included a cup. I pulled it out, but before I could get to the pail, dozens of hands already clung to the rim. Elbows were pushing, cups and bottles clinking, and in their haste, more water was spilled on the floor than was ladled out. I shed my reserve and vigorously pushed my cup into the pail. I steadied my wrist with my other hand and managed to extricate my cup, three-quarters filled, without spilling a drop. Thank Heaven for our place near the door; I didn't have to step over anybody's feet.

The pails were empty now. My mother carefully took the cup from my hand, bent over one of the pails and washed her hands. I did the same with the little that was left. Our neighbors looked surprised. "Why didn't you drink it?" they asked.

"First we had to wash our hands. There wasn't any left to drink."

They shook their heads, unable to understand.

The pails were taken away and the door closed. For the second time, we heard the clanking of our train's wheels as it moved. The train moved slowly, carefully, like a thief with stolen goods. After only a short while, it stopped. Again there was some tugging and pushing, and then all was quiet. A young woman looked out one of the windows.

"Oh, look there!" she exclaimed. "They've unhooked the

locomotive, and we are quite far from the station. They've put us on a side track. It seems we're not going to leave today!"

I couldn't see what difference it made. In any case, we were locked in, trapped in a cage. I couldn't eat. My mother took a few bites of some food, wrapped up the rest and put it back in the bag.

"I don't think it will spoil," she said. "It's cold here."

It *was* cold. Stuffy, but cold. It was hard to tell if the cold was real, though, or the kind that comes from within. I felt cut off from every life-sustaining source. The helplessness and the unknown chilled my blood. The Soviet people had experience being shipped by the hundreds of thousands from one place to another, but for us, it was something we still couldn't grasp.

The children, awakened by the commotion caused by the water, were crying again.

One pretty, little blond girl, about a year-and-a-half old, kept crying and repeating, like a broken record, "Mama, mimi mama, mimi."

"She wants milk," her mother explained.

As this was her entire vocabulary, and milk might as well have been somewhere on the moon, this cry was our constant background music in our mobile prison.

People say time is a healer, but time can be cruel as well. I looked at my watch. It was only three o'clock in the afternoon. When had they pushed us into the train cars? This morning, a month ago, a year ago? So many emotions overlapped! Despair, resignation, hope. Maybe I'd meet my father. Maybe they'd bring us to the same place where they took the prisoners.

I told my mother about the disturbing dream in which my father had appeared to me. She looked at me with her sad, beautiful, dark, wide open eyes, and her only comment was, "It is a very unusual dream." My mother always spoke little, but she could express more in a few words than others could in long speeches.

Indeed, this wasn't the only time I felt in some way actually connected to my father. The intense pain I always carried in my heart seemed more a reflection of his suffering than an expression of my own sense of loss.

CHAPTER 5

---■---

East to Siberia

"**L**OOK, LOOK WHAT'S GOING ON OUTSIDE!" CRIED ONE woman who had been keeping watch at the little windows. I jumped to my feet and pushed my head under somebody's elbow to get a better look.

A chorus of far-off voices became more audible each moment, and a mass of people exploded like pent-up steam from behind the station and started running toward our train. It seemed they had been waiting a long time and just now were allowed to approach us. Men and women of all ages were running alongside the train, calling out names. Hundreds of names. Family names, first names, a cacophony of names and voices. Faces flushed, hands waving, desperate looks. Many stopped, evidently spotting those they sought, while others kept running.

I pushed my head further out the window, and I saw my cousin Shulem. He saw me, waved his hand and ran toward our car. At a distance behind him were his parents Uncle Shmuel and Aunt Etie. They stopped in front of the window, as did relatives of some of our fellow passengers. I saw my aunt and uncle moving their lips, but the pushing inside and the noise outside made it impossible to hear. I saw Shulem pointing to the setting sun and then at his wristwatch. I took it as a sign that they had found out that the train would soon depart.

Surprisingly, the guards were indifferent to all that was going on. Watchful and stony-faced, as usual, but not interfering. Here and there, I noticed a small package or a bag being thrown into some of the windows. As it became darker, the crowd started to thin out, and the noise subsided. My uncle and aunt left, but Shulem stayed nearby.

"Stay near the window, I'll be back soon," I could hear him say distinctly. Then I understood what he had actually meant by pointing at the setting sun–they would be back after *Shabbos*.

The "soon" took about two hours. They returned loaded with packages. I wondered how they had managed to carry so much. Though our train was far out on a side track, it was illuminated by the guards' searchlights. Shulem was seventeen years old at the time, strong and very tall. Fearing that the guards might change their minds, he started to throw one package after another through our window with lightning speed and impressive aim. I stood a bit back in the car catching them in the air so they wouldn't fall on anyone inside. When I had deposited the last package, I looked out to thank him, but he and my aunt and uncle were already far from our car, probably hurried away by the guard. There weren't any other people around.

Shortly after, the water procedure started again. It was very welcome, and this time it was shared in a more orderly manner. But again, even though we drank our whole share besides a few drops to wash our fingers, it was not enough.

Soon, we had our first real taste of Soviet dehumanization. We were so shocked and humiliated that the only appreciation we could have for the "service" was that the first ordeal prepared us for those to come. Each car carried an average of two-and-a-half to three dozen adults. From each car, in groups of four accompanied by one of the guards (the other was watching the car door), we were led by the guard's bayonet down to the train tracks to answer nature's call. Even a dog on a leash is not hurried by its master. We were. And at close range. Later, the cattle cars would often stop just before reaching a station or right after leaving it for the same purpose, or more often, the procedure was carried out with our train on a side track.

We had to go through the same torment throughout the whole stretch of our route, twice a day, in the morning and in the evening. By Stalin's will, our systems had to be conditioned to meet this schedule. With one pail emptied twice a day, and six children on board, we adults did our best to cooperate with his decree. It was an order which made for a foul-smelling train car and no peace of mind, followed by a respite totally squelched by disgrace and disgust.

It was cold in the car, and we sat with our coats on. A dim light from a kerosene lantern, hung from the ceiling, transformed our heads, hands and bodies into long, scary shadows and filled the air with smoky fumes. Some were sleeping and even snoring, some sitting bent and dozing, others wide awake and looking at the ceiling and the flickering light. I arranged our bundles as comfortably as possible, so my mother could have some semblance of a cot. Hours passed, but my mother and I were unable to sleep. At the end of the night, a slight slumber overwhelmed me, but it was soon interrupted by the early morning routine.

The new day found our train on the same side track on which we'd been left the night before. My cousin Shulem was back again. Besides the monotonous pounding of the guards' boots, there was complete silence, and at once, I recognized Shulem's voice calling my name.

I looked out and caught a bundle. Two more were lying on the ground. He was alone. The bundles were small, tightly packed to be able to pass through the window. It was about a kilometer and a half from their house to the station, and he made many trips there and back loaded with packages. Much later, when I opened them, I found items which had been in the boxes we had left with our friends. Evidently, Etie and Shmuel were busy recovering them. The practical Etie remembered to include two big burlap sacks and a colored tablecloth, so I would be able to make a few big bundles from all the small packages. On one small package was written a note, "Eat it at once, it will get spoiled." We "ate" more than once from this package, which contained money in rectangular bundles, neatly wrapped in handkerchiefs and tied with thread. They were sandwiched between two towels. We hid them securely.

The morning passed without incident. At noon, a plain wooden crate filled with brick-like loaves of black bread was placed on the floor near the door with the guard's dry order, "Divide in even portions among yourselves."

During our journey, the bread delivery was erratic. The first few days, it didn't matter. Almost everyone in the wagon had enough to eat. The only exception was the poor peasant woman whom we all helped out as best we could, sharing what we had.

Late in the afternoon on the second day of our stay on the side track in Lida, our train awakened from its lethargy. Shaking, screeching and clanking, it moved back to the main track, further away from the station.

People from town found out, and I saw them gathered into a sea of human heads and waving hands. They had been permitted to come to the station, but they had not been permitted to come close to the train. I couldn't understand why the N.K.V.D. was making such a spectacle of the whole thing. Usually, such acts were performed secretly under the cover of night. But since tyranny had become a virtue, I believe it was done to inflict more suffering on the families who were left behind.

The crying and wailing of the human mass at the station drowned out our train's whistle announcing our departure. The locomotive moved slowly, and the wails outside penetrated every fiber of my body and soul until I felt thoroughly numb. I stood watching the receding station and the receding mass of people, until they faded into a colorless blur.

It seemed unbelievable, but I slept through the night. When I woke up, it was bright daylight. The train was stationary. I looked out and saw a passenger train facing ours. It was blocking the station building, so I couldn't see the name of the town we were in. One of the passengers in a window looked familiar. Yes, it was Kushner, the attorney from Lida. We recognized each other in spite of my tiny window, and he was close enough to ask me what had happened to us. Kushner had been away from home for a few days, and as our deportation was the first from Lida, he had no notion of what had been going on.

The station was Baranovich, he told me, a well-known Lithuanian town, and his passenger train was going in the opposite direction from ours. I asked him to tell my uncles he had seen me. Much later, my aunts wrote that the same day he had given them regards.

Another day passed, and we reached the city of Brest-Litovsk. Here again, we went through the same routine of moving the train back and forth between the main track and a side track.

The train was kept on a side track all day, and late at night, after the familiar maneuvering, pushing and pulling, we were told to transfer to another train, a Russian one. Our first train had been of Polish manufacture, and the Polish cars didn't fit the Russian tracks.

The operation was carried out in the characteristic Soviet manner. We were awakened late at night, without advance notice, and mercilessly rushed. Disoriented children were crying as heavy bundles were thrown out of the car, one upon the other, and left for us to drag to the next train. The Russian cars were dirty, with a dusty, moldy smell and cracks between the boards on the floor and the walls and bars on the windows. But they had one advantage—they had bunks.

The lantern swinging from the ceiling provided hardly any light, and it was impossible to sort out the bundles. Exhausted, indifferent and resigned, we climbed onto the bare bunks.

That night was *Pesach*. No wine, no *seder*, no *Haggadah*. Just reclining on our bundles among the Poles. *Pesach*, the symbol of freedom; the turning point in our fate as a nation; our transition from slaves into a free people who were given the choice and privilege to accept the greatest gift ever bestowed by Hashem–the holy Torah. *Pesach* was to be spent in Soviet bondage surrounded by filth.

Among the parcels brought by my cousin Shulem were some *Pesach* dishes. The most useful was an enamel, quart-size container with a lid and a handle to be carried as a little pail. It came in very handy during our long trip.

My mother and I didn't have our first taste of Soviet bread until about twelve days later. The first few days, our meals consisted of two or three bites at a time. Our throats were constricted, unable to swallow. Then, during the eight days of *Pesach*, we ate *matzoh* with water. I made a deal with the other women in the car. They could have our two portions of bread, and all of our leftover *chametz*, in exchange for letting us take two cups of water first, before they dunked their *chametzdicke* cups into the pail. They agreed and the deal was honored.

The next day, our train passed the old Russian-Polish border. The difference was striking. Although in comparison with western Poland, our region was considered a back country, after a century and a half of Czarist rule, the Russian countryside presented a far more pathetic sight. The long rows of freshly plowed soil and neat little houses with fenced gardens in our part of Poland, contrasted sharply with the overall neglect on the Russian side. The fields, villages and houses looked dried up from a flood–colorless, lifeless and sad. The train passed through vast stretches of Soviet territory, and everywhere, the view was the same. We had embarked on a road paved with ice.

Our cars were still locked. They were opened only for the deliveries of water or bread, or when the group "excursions" took place. They first let us out without close security only after we passed Kiev, in the Ukraine. There, they were sure we would not run away. Earlier, there had already been a few cases of people escaping. Later in Siberia, I met two families whose daughter and two young sons had escaped during the group "convenience" trips. But this was when we were still close to home. Now, deep into Russian territory, none of us had any incentive to attempt it.

Halfway out of Poland, there was a memorable occasion. Our train stopped at an obscure, large station, with many crisscrossing tracks. The doors were flung open, and our guard called out, "*Vagon lavka*! Train store! If anyone wants to buy some food, go quickly to the last car on your left!"

We had left Lida two weeks before. Our daily rations consisted of bread and water. Just two weeks! How adaptable human nature is! We had already become used to our chains. Now, to be allowed to leave the train and buy whatever we wanted? It seemed too good to be true.

In the rush and excitement and the semi-darkness of the car, I put on two different shoes, a beige one of mine and a brown one of my mother's. Running to the *lavka*, I didn't notice the difference until someone pulled my sleeve.

"I see you have two pairs of shoes," a Russian woman was saying. "Will you sell me one pair?"

She was wearing some kind of uniform, and I assumed she was a train dispatcher or some other type of station attendant.

"*Proday, proday*" she persisted. "Sell, sell."

I heard these words hundreds of times during the time I spent in Russia, but this first encounter gave me a beginning of an understanding of the way people there were forced to live.

On the way to the store car and standing in line, I met many women and girls I knew from Lida and the exclamation, "You, too?" rang in all directions. Until then, the deportees in one car hadn't known who was in the next.

There wasn't much to buy at the store. The few candies, the single can of tomato sauce and the very salty, dry herring they allotted each person couldn't be called a bargain, but just to be able to walk the length of the train and meet acquaintances and friends and exchange a few words was a refreshing and encouraging change–a balm to our atrophied limbs and minds.

"*Pa vagonam*! Into the wagons!" The call brought our brief respite to an abrupt end.

The train moved, and by reading the names of the stations we passed, we knew we were going east. I can't recall any more *lavka* stops, but we were let out to fetch water at certain stations, in groups accompanied by the guards. Our train made fewer prolonged stops now, and one morning when it stopped at Ufa, we noticed from afar a chain of mountains enveloped in a pinkish gray fog, like a vast curtain of ice. We were nearing the Urals. Siberia lay beyond.

Siberia, the valley of tears, the graveyard of thousands of tortured victims of maniacal, tyrannical whims. Siberia, a vast expanse of extremely fertile soil, thousands of miles of forests, coal mines, steppes, tundra and natural resources. Where mismanagement, lack of organization and initiative, and plain neglect had put to waste Heaven-sent riches, the Soviets now expected to exploit these riches by harnessing human robots, helpless, weak, hungry captives quartered in barely inhabitable holes. The captives would be forced to work until they dropped. There were plenty of red cattle cars to bring more.

When we passed the Ural Mountains, the natural border between Europe and Asia, one of the women in our car remarked, "I feel like I'm going to my own funeral."

Many agreed, but this was not my feeling. My mother took it all with great strength and equanimity, saying, "If this is the Almighty's will, we are not supposed to complain."

The Polish women couldn't understand her philosophy. They lacked the tempering the Jewish people have had in a long history of pogroms and suffering. The arrogant Polish anti-Semites of yesterday had just lost their country and, with it, their pride and beliefs. It seemed there was nothing left for them to hold onto. They looked with surprise at my mother. So fragile, eating so little, but so strong morally. It's been said, "The same fire that melts butter hardens steel." The fire of belief and trust in Heaven permits a hope, which in turn gives the strength to overcome situations which otherwise would be unendurable.

I, too, looked with admiration at my mother. In moments when my spirits sank, my mother's words lifted my mood. "Dina'le, have *bitachon*. Hashem can reverse the *gezeirah*, and we have to believe He will. Do not despair."

"Yes, Mama, I will be strong for you and Papa," I would reply.

In the long hours on the Russian train, the women developed a certain camaraderie. There was nothing to do; we hadn't packed books or knitting. When the shock wore off, after the first few days, they mostly took to talking, telling stories of what they had lost and of how they had come to be deported. My mother refrained from almost all conversation. She had never been one for talking, and now she clung to her *Tehillim*, most of which she knew by heart.

Most of the women were quite intelligent and well-educated. Their husbands were the higher officials in the town and the intelligentsia, which is how they had come to be arrested and their families deported. In Poland, their high class had only made them snobbish. One woman I recognized from before had been the postmistress in Lida, an offensive anti-Semite. Now, having lost everything, they lost their pride as well, and many actually became considerate of even the poorest of the poor Poles in our car, and courteous to my mother and myself, as well.

I was neither interested in listening nor in talking, though their conversation often interrupted my thoughts. Our adverse circumstances, and as always my father's arrest and his undoubted suffering, were so freshly painful that I was often too distraught to speak.

As desolate as the countryside was in the European part, it was even more so in the Asiatic part of Russia. The only advantage we could see was that now our door was not locked. As we neared our destination, the water supply became very erratic. Then one day, water wasn't brought at all. We were told that the station where we had stopped couldn't spare any drinking water for our train. Thirst is more painful than hunger. Our thirst was exacerbated by the dry and salty herring, which had become a regular addition to our bread rations.

In Siberia, snow is not a rarity in May. It was melting now, leaving big puddles, which in some places looked like small lakes. We saw large stretches of land along our way, covered with marshes and puddles. As the second day came and again there was no water, we decided to take advantage of the puddles. When our train stopped in the middle of nowhere, as happened often enough with the human cargo trains which had no regular schedule, many took pitchers, pails or bowls in hand and carefully climbed down, as the water reached the base of the embankment. My little enamel pail came in very handy now.

Coming back into the car with the treasured liquid, we had quite a disappointment. An assortment of whirling and curling creatures was distinctly visible at the bottom of our pails. Many people in our car drank the water after straining it through a handkerchief. I also strained ours, but we used it only to wash our hands. The lack of water was extremely painful, but here again, patience and will power helped out. That evening, water was delivered, and a few stops later, in Chelyabinsk, we were taken to the station pump and permitted to drink our fill.

At the end of the first week of May, we arrived at a place called Tokushy. It was a big and empty station, colorless and lifeless. Attached to the station building with a separate entrance was a huge room where we were told to bring our bundles. Alongside it was another smaller room, resembling some kind of an office for the N.K.V.D., who now replaced the guards.

No gourmet dinner was prepared for our arrival, not even the claylike, odd-tasting, bluish-gray bread. There was water; we were told there was a pump at the station, and later in the evening, we could get *kipiatok* (boiling water) at the station's tea room. We had already forgotten the taste of something warm.

CHAPTER 6

■

New Migrations

In the intervening chapters of the full, unabridged edition, the author and her mother are confronted by the harsh realities of life in Siberia. In this chapter, they can already look at new arrivals through "veteran" eyes.

ONE MORNING AT THE END OF MARCH, 1944, OUR VILLAGE awoke to a deluge of strange-looking people literally taking up every available space. There were tall men in long, black sheepskin coats and huge fur hats like overturned pails, and women in balloon pants under tiers of multicolored skirts, with short, quilted, multicolored jackets, heads covered with two or three shawls, one on top of the other.

The Soviets are marvelously efficient at uprooting people, plucking them like weeds and depositing them in far-off places among unfamiliar surroundings. In this case, a whole tribe called Tchetchentzy, numbering five hundred thousand people, were given the customary fifteen-minute notice, taken forcibly from their homes, loaded into wagons and brought to Siberia. The reason was alleged disloyalty to the Soviet Union. They were dispersed over Northern Kazakhstan to be settled there for good. They were to receive some assistance from the government—a piece of land to build a house on and one cow per family.

They were a Muslim tribe who had been living from time immemorial in the Caucasus Mountains near the Black Sea. Adhering to their ancient customs, they grazed their flocks of sheep on the slopes of the mountains, and their women, like their forebears for generations before them, carried water in tall, beautifully carved silver jugs on their heads.

Their houses and flocks of sheep had all been confiscated, and the most that some of them had managed to take in the allotted fifteen minutes were their distinctive fur hats, their elaborate silver link belts studded with rhinestones and their daggers with elaborate silver handles, items traditionally passed on from father to son for generations. The women took their collections of colored skirts and silver jugs.

While the resettling was being arranged, those brought to Tokushy were packed into all the government buildings, schools, warehouses, the railroad station and even barns. They stayed for a month, until they were sent to various *kolkhozy*. The crowded, unhygienic conditions bred disease, and a typhus epidemic broke out among them, which spread rapidly among the local people. Typhus had been unknown before in the cold Siberian climate. The epidemic took many lives, among them our dear Dr. Zaira. No other doctor was sent to Tokushy after her death.

One year earlier, three hundred thousand Germans, who had been living in Russia in the Volga region for centuries, were also brought in a similar manner to Siberia, the dumping ground for all undesirables. The Volgas were not trusted, so with the advance of the Nazi army, they were moved elsewhere. Some of them stayed for a short time in Tokushy, en route to further regions. I remember one distinctly. He was a deposed K.G.B. official, still wearing his K.G.B. uniform, the long coat, but without the buttons, with the shoulder straps ripped off at one end swinging loosely, reminding him with each flap of his lost devil's paradise. On his head, he still wore the green banded cap, without its horrific emblem and star. Good for him, I thought, and wished that all K.G.B. would look like this one.

Meanwhile, the winter of 1944 neared its end. With the Almighty's help and my mother's own strong will and boundless faith, she overcame the pneumonia, and when *Pesach* came, she had recovered completely.

Pesach brought some joy. Even in Siberia, we shook ourselves loose from our continual misery in honor of *Yom Tov*. Every year we renewed our unshakable faith that "*leshanah habaah bnei chorin*; next year we shall be free."

Before we had a chance to begin deliberating amongst ourselves about whether or not we wanted to risk baking *matzos* again, Brodatch brought us *matzos* from Petropavlovsk. We were astounded. Where had he gotten them? The answer surprised us even more. They were Manischewitz *matzos*! He had bought them on the black market. They had originally come from the Joint Distribution Committee in America, which had been allowed to open a "Jewish Committee" in Moscow through the International Red Cross after the Allies had joined Russia in the war. Since the receipt of the Polish shipment a year before, this was the first sign we had of contact with the Allies. I had no idea how the *matzos* had gotten onto the black market, but it didn't matter. It was a touch of the free world. There were people who knew about us and cared! Even the blue and yellow colored wrappers were exciting.

Brodatch offered them to us for his cost price, and we bought one package. It contained ten or twelve *matzos*, barely enough for the nights of *Yom Tov* and *Shabbos*. We also had no wine, *marror* or *Haggados*, so our *seudas Yom Tov* seemed more like a potato supper than a *seder*. But we sang whatever we remembered, told the story of *yetzias Mitzrayim* as best we could and prayed that *leshanah habaah b'Yerushalayim* (next year in Jerusalem) and that we should be able to observe *Pesach* with all its practices and not just with our hearts.

CHAPTER 7

---◼---

Culture, Siberian Style

ONE THING WHICH MADE WORK IN THE *ARTEL* A BIT more bearable were the radio speakers hung up high on one wall in our work room. The *artel* was one of the few establishments in Tokushy which had electricity (there were outlets provided only for the speakers). These weren't regular radios with dials and separate stations, only speakers like inverted plates. Whatever was broadcast on the one official station was what we had to listen to. Mostly, it was a constant flow of propaganda or music, but it was still a link with the outside world.

The war was still raging. When the going was rough, they played loud and happy music to mislead the people and keep the morale high. When the enemy was beaten, we heard high-spirited propaganda. There were no other clues as to the real

76

situation. At times, when the Soviet army recaptured an important town and pushed the German army back, the music and propaganda would be interrupted with an announcement that such and such a city was liberated. We were shocked to find out that the Germans had penetrated so deeply into Russian territory.

About two weeks before *Pesach*, the *artel* manager asked me to knit a sweater which he intended to send to Petropavlovsk to the yearly exhibition of the products of the more competitive *artels* in Northern Kazakhstan. "Make something special, and after the exhibition is over, you'll get the sweater as a present," he said. I did, indeed, get a present out of it, but not quite as the manager had promised.

Since he had asked me for something special, I realized how badly he wanted his *artel* to excel. Though a large part of my earnings were spent on supplying him with vodka, I had to consider how much I had benefitted from him. I was spared the coal mines, I was able to observe *Shabbos*, I wasn't separated from my mother, and I had many other benefits. I felt the manager deserved my best effort. I asked him to allow me to knit at home so that the wool would stay clean and to give me one week, as for any other sweater. He agreed. I chose the finest, purest white wool and decided to crochet a lacy design. I also decided to make it in a large size, because I knew that, regardless of his promise, the sweater would go to some official's wife who was probably on the heavy side. I must admit it came out special. It drew many ooh's and aah's when I brought the finished product to the *artel*.

A week later, it was on display at the exhibition, along with their usual merchandise like *pimy*, axes, barrels, quilted army pants and jackets. It was the only *kulturny* item there, to use the words of Shura, the warehouse manager. The new rulers of Siberia had come from the lower classes, and they loved to apply high-sounding labels to anything with the slightest sophistication. The word *kulturny*, meaning cultured, had a special attraction. Every town had a park for "culture and rest." For recreation, there were a few half-broken benches, and culture was usually represented by a *kiosk*, a stand selling not newspapers and magazines but beer. For those lucky ones who were first in line, it often ended in drunken brawls, leaving bleeding noses and purple eyes. Culture, Siberian style.

The manager of my *artel* had his moment of triumph, and the *kulturny* sweater contributed to it. The wife of a juror probably admired it and the *artel*, for the first time, won the citation for "higher achievement."

There is, however, no place for joy in Russia. Evidently, some other *artel* also wanted the citation, and jealousy is a dangerous weapon there. A wink, a word, and somebody's head falls. About a week after the exhibition ended, when we came to work in the morning, a short, stocky man in a military uniform, with buttons and shoulder straps missing, appeared before us, introducing himself as the new manager of the *artel*.

Nobody asks questions in Russia. But sometimes, answers present themselves without asking. Observing our new manager, we noticed two things—the missing buttons and the flapping shoulder straps, both of which did not attest to an honorable discharge. Even in the middle of a raging war, the slightest transgression could cause a high-ranking military man to be removed from the army. As he probably hadn't been able to obtain a civilian suit, he had no choice but to wear the evidence of his disgrace. The cut and material of his uniform indicated a higher rank, so the job as an *artel* manager in Siberia must have been his exile and punishment.

To rehabilitate himself in the eyes of the authorities, the new manager went to the utmost extreme in strictness and zeal. From the first day, I realized that the vodka business was finished. It wouldn't work with this manager. The *artel* sweater orders also came to an abrupt end. I went back to the socks and mittens. At the end of the first week, on Friday at sunset, I took some yarn and went home as usual. Sunday morning, I brought the finished quota. No reprimand, no being called to the office. I didn't know what to expect, and I was afraid to approach him. I was sure his strictness wouldn't tolerate my independence.

By then, I knew the general rule that wives can influence their husbands. More than once I had used the back door method for one thing or another; why not try now? In his zeal to prove himself, the new manager would remain in the office long after the workers had gone, and this gave me the opportunity to go see his wife.

I had seen her once in the street. She was an attractive, urban-looking woman, not the Siberian village type. I took a pair of my good, high-heeled shoes, the likes of which had long not been seen in Russia, even in Moscow before the war, and went to her house. They lived not far from us. She was a good housekeeper and had already transformed her plain village hut into a cozy home, with white curtains, a few pictures on the walls and a lot of needlework. She was thrilled with the shoes and tried them on. They were just her size. When she asked the price, I told her I was a worker in the *artel*, and this was a present for a good start in her new home. She was very excited and said she was really glad to meet such a nice person in Tokushy. She asked where I lived and promised to visit me and reciprocate with one of her needlepoints.

Evidently, when her husband came home, he didn't share her enthusiasm, because the next day when I returned from work, I found the shoes lying on my trunk. My heart sank. My mother didn't make any remarks. She never liked to discuss unpleasant things. Etia and Kreina were also silent.

At the *artel* the next day, it was business as usual. The new manager used to go through the different departments several times a day, which the previous one seldom did. When he came into our room, I kept my eyes on my work and didn't see his expression. On Friday, I did the same as always. Sunday at noon, the girl from the office appeared at the door and called out, "Dina, go to the manager." I didn't expect to hear compliments from him, but I also wasn't prepared to see a policeman with a rifle.

When they're sent as *politruks* to indoctrinate, they can spill hundreds of words a minute, but when they're sent from the K.G.B. with rifles, the Soviet policemen become mute. I knew a question wouldn't be answered, so instead of asking I said, "I want to let my mother know."

"You come with me. You are under arrest."

The girl from the office brought my sweater. I wasn't even allowed to go back to the room where I worked.

My mother didn't have to wait until the evening to find out. Kreina, a half-liter bottle of milk in her hand, was returning from some "business deal." She saw me being led into the street by the K.G.B.

The K.G.B. man brought me to the train station, looked at the clock on the wall and remained mute. I knew our destination was Poludieno, home of the local K.G.B., the police station and the prison. After fifteen minutes, a passenger train arrived. The policeman showed a paper to the conductor, who respectfully let us enter the car.

A half-hour later, I was led through a long and narrow hall to a small cell. A rifle-bearing soldier opened the big, rusty lock. I stepped quietly inside and the door closed behind me. The cell was barely five feet wide by ten feet long, and all it contained was a narrow, three-foot wooden bench, a small, barred window on the far wall, directly under the ceiling, and next to the door, a tin pail. A burning bulb was suspended on a wire, and there was no switch inside the cell. I sat down on the bench, leaned against the wall, looked at my watch and closed my eyes.

CHAPTER 8

■

Arrest and Interrogation

M Y FATHER! HOW MANY DAYS, NIGHTS, MONTHS HAD HE sat in similar isolation in a prison cell? I looked again at my watch. It struck me that it had been a present from my father on my fourteenth birthday, a small, excellent, gold Longines. Even the original band was still intact. How was it that I hadn't thought about it all these years? I pressed it to my heart. My father had held it in his hand. I thought about his joy when he bought it, his joy when he gave it to me. The cell disappeared. I was with my father again, feeling his soft, brown eyes looking at me, his warm, reassuring smile.

Yes, Papa, I promised silently, I will not disappoint you, I'll try to be strong. But don't leave me. You always cared so much. You knew my every wish, my every thought, as I knew yours. My yearning and longing to see you, to hear your voice, transcended the hundreds or maybe thousands of kilometers that lay between us. They reached you, I know, as yours reached me.

Papa, for over a year now, I haven't felt the intense pain I had the first three years. I felt when your *heilige neshamah* went to heaven, when your suffering ended. Hashem has compassionately freed you from the confines of the Soviet prison and the pain they inflicted upon you.

You fulfilled your share of *mitzvos* and *tzeddakah* which you gave with so much warmth and readiness. Your sensitivity to the needs of others had no equal. It was a *zchus* to be endowed with a nature like yours. It was Hashem's gift to you. And you worked on yourself to bring it to the highest perfection. Why didn't I write down and learn by heart all those things you taught me, how you dealt with people. Did I learn enough? Papa, I know you see me now. I have *bitachon*, Papa, just as you always had.

My gaze wandered to the little window. It was grayish-blue now, not the light yellow it had been when I entered. I realized I was still pressing my hand with the watch to my heart. My hand had fallen asleep, and now it stung when I moved it.

Was it possible? I thought. Had I been sitting here for four hours? Yes, it was six o'clock now.

From the hall, I heard the monotonous, measured steps of the sentry. Four steps forward, four steps back. Had he been there all the time? I looked at the length of my cell and realized I would also be able to take four steps. I picked myself up, stood for a while, went to the door and back to the bench. All of a sudden, I felt drained and hungry. The bench was hard and narrow, the wall felt cold, the bulb too strong and too low for such a small area. I was thankful that at least I didn't suffer from claustrophobia.

Time was passing. The little window became black now. My head started to throb, and I tried not to think. I just sat with my legs stretched out. I turned my head to one side, then to the other. There was no escape from the glaring bulb. I wanted to move the bench away a little, but it was fastened to the floor. I stopped looking at my watch. Time seems to slow its pace when checked too often. I just sat glued to the bench, atrophied and numb. I felt my inner tension, discomfort, exhaustion and hunger disappear. Everything vanished. I fell asleep.

A sharp screech from the lock and the sentry's voice woke me. "*Zavut k natchalniku*," he said. "You are called to the supervisor."

I jumped to my feet. Reality started to dawn. My watch told me it was one o'clock in the morning. I had often heard from surviving prisoners that K.G.B. interrogations are always in the middle of the night, when alertness and resistance are at their lowest. It's easier to break a person's will, even make him admit crimes he never committed, when he is disoriented. I went to the door, blurry-eyed, stepped into the hall and started walking. The soldier with the rifle directed me from behind. One turn, then another, all on the same floor in the same building.

"*Zdyes*," he said. "Here it is."

I saw a bright beam of light from an open door forming a rectangle on the floor, and I entered. A huge oak desk stood on a Persian carpet in the middle of the room, flanked by four upholstered chairs. I regained my full awareness and took in every detail. Against the wall to the right were bookcases filled with folders of varying thicknesses. To the left stood a couch. On the wall opposite the door, next to a large clock was the familiar portrait of the tyrant Stalin. There was no desk lamp, only a light fixture with bright milkglass bulbs hanging above the desk.

Three chairs were occupied. Facing the door was the K.G.B. head, in a very regal uniform and cap, to his right, a stenographer with a pad and pencil in hand, and to his left, another K.G.B. man leafing through a three-inch thick folder. Both of the K.G.B. officers were in uniform but capless. The *natchalnik* had all the usual desk accessories in front of him, plus a pistol on each side of the desk pad. I was calm enough to wonder if he shot his prisoners with both hands at once. On a small table near the bookcases was a telephone, the first and last one I saw in Siberia.

He motioned to the chair opposite him, and I sat down; the soldier with the rifle remained at the door. He gave me a quick look, verified my name and, pointing to the thick folder, said, "You see, this is your case. You'll have to answer for all your crimes."

I heard what he said, saw the folder, but somehow remained detached, as if it were not my fate that was at stake. Thoughts flew through my head. How could I remain so calm? Was I really sitting here? Or was I still in my cell? Then I remembered that I had promised my father to be strong, not to disappoint him.

He leaned back, both hands on the arms of his chair as a signal for the assistant to take over. The assistant opened the folder, turning page after page, shaking his head, his expression changing from horror to wonder, with an occasional "tsk! tsk!" as if lost in an ocean of crime, not knowing where to begin.

Finally, he stopped leafing, slapped the open folder,

raised his eyes and fixed them on me.

"Do you know what sabotage in wartime means?"

This question was followed by a litany of paragraphs and articles and the punishment they entailed. The list of crimes was long. The weekly prayer gatherings in our house which were illegal, counterrevolutionary and severely punishable. My leaving work on my own every week for religious purposes, one of the most blatant offenses, which set a bad example to one hundred and eighty workers, all producing army articles, and could be understood only as provocation to revolt and sabotage. The *matzoh* baking, which was considered "commercial activity." He read on, page after page, citing the grave punishment for each crime separately. The stenographer was busy flashing his pencil, interrupting briefly to turn a page.

The litany over, he stopped and closed the file. The *natchalnik* remained silent the whole time, but his cold, piercing look did not leave my face. He was planning his strategy according to my expression. He expected panic, fear and confusion. My face didn't register any of these. As he remained silent, I assumed he was waiting for some explanation on my part. The calm didn't leave me, and in a quiet but firm voice, I started to refute point by point the accusations leveled against me. He let me talk for about ten minutes and then, all of a sudden, raised his fist and let it fall on his desk with a powerful thud, causing the inkwell, pens and pistols to jump.

"Enough! Stop! I know your kind!" he roared.

Hashem gave me courage. By no means could I have mastered it myself. His tactic was calculated. I remained calm. After a few minutes of silence, he took one of the pens, started to play with it, moved his chair to the desk, leaned both elbows on it and the mask of a wild beast turned into the mask of a smiling gentleman. The stenographer was ready to start, he knew the order of business.

Still playing with the pen, the *natchalnik* began in a confidential, fatherly tone. "You heard the accusations against you. They are facts, and no explanation will alter them. You'll get a long prison term with hard labor in one of the Arctic labor camps. We know that your mother is sick and depends on you. You will never see your mother again. It is wartime now, and regulations are strict." He stopped for a while, then continued. "There is one way out for you, though, and I will use my influence to help you. It is very simple. You will work for us. You know Polish, Russian, Yiddish and German. All you have to do is listen to what people say, and once a month, you'll come here with a report. You'll be paid very well, and you'll get the best rations."

He was smiling, assured that the prospect of well-being would be tempting in comparison with the severe punishment he had detailed. He didn't expect my categorical "No!"

"What? You refuse? You'll be very sorry!" He opened the drawer of his desk, took out a paper, held it up high, repeated more of what he had said before and added, "Just sign it, and in the morning you can go home worry-free."

I tried to appear simple-minded and kept repeating, "No, no, I am not good at it. Besides, I am a sleep-talker. We live together with two other families; in my sleep I might tell what I'm doing, and then people will avoid me and not talk around me. What good will it do?"

He gave me a sharp look. "Whom do you think you're fooling? We are not here to play around. Either you sign or you are arrested."

"I will not sign. I will not become a spy."

The expression on his face became an interplay of masks—wild rage to scare me, smiling politeness to subdue me. I remained unbending.

It was four o'clock in the morning when the sentry locked my cell door from the outside. I went to my bench and fell asleep immediately. The screech from the lock woke me up. The door opened a little. A pint size tin cup of milk, on top of it a pita bread and a tin jug of water were placed on the floor near the door. The pail was taken away and in a few minutes brought back. It was seven a.m. I washed my hands, said *Modeh Ani* and, like a desert wanderer, couldn't satiate my thirst until the jug was three-quarters empty. The milk and the pita were the only food for the day. I didn't touch them.

During the five days and four nights I was incarcerated, I drank only the water. Each morning, a fresh cup of milk and pita were placed on the floor and yesterday's taken away uneaten. I wanted the K.G.B. head to know that the hunger strike was an expression of my determination, but at the subsequent audiences, he never mentioned it. I suspected that the sentry ate the food himself and didn't report it to him.

I was probably in a special category. Who had ever heard of prisoners being fed milk and pitas? True, it was only once a day, but it was still a treat, a treat to tempt me into the trap. It was still early morning. I knew that during the day I would be left alone. Alone, yes, but watched. The door had a tiny opening with a sliding panel outside. Many times during the day I heard the sound of it moving and even caught sight of the sentry's eye and a part of his forehead.

The tightly wound coil in me from the night before started to unwind. I sat on the bench, the thoughts trapped in my head vying for priority. One thing I knew for sure—I would not agree to become an informer. A *moser*? Even if my very life were at stake, it was only one life. How many lives would I endanger by becoming a *moser*? My saintly mother would understand. Not a word of *lashon hora* had passed her lips since I could remember. To talk about anyone in general was taboo in our house. My parents adhered to the rules of *shmiras halashon* totally. Should I now break them? And in such a way? Never! I knew it would be very hard to withstand their pressure, their tricks, the threats which they might carry out at any moment. The K.G.B. head had his superior in Petropavlovsk, who in turn had his superior in Moscow. Each of them wanted to prove his efficiency. Spying, terrorizing, arresting and torturing were the tools that made the regime tick. But come what may, my decision was firm. I prayed to the Almighty that He help me be strong, not to waver even for a moment.

I knew what had happened to two people who preceded me. I knew them very well. One was a woman from Poludieno, a mother of two young girls whose husband had just been released from prison. Unable to withstand the pressure, she agreed to become an informer. Shortly afterwards, she was taken to the hospital after suffering a nervous breakdown. The K.G.B. then "invited" to their office a middle-aged man who, together with his wife, had been deported to Siberia. He was a sickly person and after returning from the K.G.B. office in Poludieno, openly admitted his failure to stand up to the K.G.B. His words on return were, "I have one request from the Almighty—that He take me before I have to go back to them." His wish was fulfilled. After two weeks, he passed away. Another Jewish grave in a Siberian cemetery.

I closed my eyes. I knew my mother was saying *Tehillim* at that moment. She did every free minute, even before I was taken to jail. Her eyes never cried, only her heart. The intensity of her prayer was very deep, even though she shed no tears.

Oh, please Almighty G-d, I prayed silently, accept our combined prayers! Hasn't it been enough until now? Enough! *Dayenu!*—a reversed *Haggadah*. Isn't it enough that my father was arrested? Isn't it enough that we were dispossessed, robbed of everything we owned? Isn't it enough that my father's *heilige neshamah* had to expire somewhere in a Siberian gulag? Isn't it enough that we don't know the date of his *yahrzeit* or the place where he is buried? Isn't it enough that we were exiled to Siberia? Isn't it enough that for a year and a half we were forced to live in tents in temperatures reaching fifty degrees below zero? I know, Hashem, that everything You do has a purpose. Am I being tested now? Please give me the strength to withstand Your test!

CHAPTER 9

―■―

An Insidious Offer

I PROBABLY DOZED OFF, BECAUSE WHEN I OPENED MY EYES, most of the day was gone. A sudden pang of hunger made my head turn involuntarily in the direction of the door. I averted it quickly. After a while, I took a few sips of water and went back to the bench. I wanted to save my energy for the midnight encounter. A surge of anger erupted suddenly in me at that K.G.B. scoundrel who justified his sitting in a warm, carpeted office by gathering information about innocent people, which was just as often invented without even any proof by the victims' envious rivals. For him and his ilk to succeed in their jobs, they would send a parent of small children to jail for imaginary crimes.

A whole sophisticated system of internal spying was invented by these moral perverts. The whole machine of the powerful K.G.B. was geared to sustain the Soviet regime through terror and fear. Teachers in grade schools were urged to extract information from students about their parents. In their innocence, unaware of the trap and wanting to please their teachers, the children told what they heard, often exaggerating as some small children might do, adding fantasy to facts. The practice became known, and parents became afraid to talk freely in front of their own children. A person couldn't even be sure of his neighbor's intentions. Co-workers didn't trust each other. Siblings were afraid to confide in each other. Everyone suspected everyone.

I didn't know what kind of persuasion or threat the *natchalnik* would try on me this time. There was no doubt he'd be persistent, determined to succeed. I decided to match wits with him, to play along with his game. But then, maybe he'd skip a day to tire me out emotionally and physically. Maybe he wouldn't call me at all.

I could recall times when there weren't enough hours in my day, but now it seemed to take endless hours to turn this day into night. Did my little watch deceive me? I took another few sips of water, stretched my aching legs and arms, leaned against the door and remained standing there for a while. If the sentry happened to open his little window, he wouldn't see too much this time. Another couple of hours passed. I was sitting on the bench again, my eyes burning from the lack of sleep and the glaring bulb.

The inquisitors knew how to torture their victims. They confined a person into a space less than three meters square with nothing but a small bench to sit on, a bulb burning day and night, scanty food and water, locked in, left to guess what the next move would be. All this was done in order to break a person and then mold him into a mindless automaton.

They didn't skip a day. At one o'clock in the morning, I was again brought into the interrogator's office. I made up my mind to remain entirely passive. Ever since I first saw a K.G.B. agent, four years earlier, walking the streets of Lida, just the sight of their uniforms used to send needles along my spine. But now, trapped in their cage, brought face to face with the harshest threats, nothing moved me. I was calm and composed. The K.G.B. head noticed it and was puzzled himself. His fox's instinct told him that screaming and fist-pounding would not convince me. Instead, he applied his eloquence. For two and a half hours, a deluge of words assured me of the bliss I would share if I would agree and the doom I'd bring down upon myself and my mother if I'd refuse. I let him talk. He stopped a few times, just to hear my firm refusal. This time, he didn't rage. He remained calm and continued talking. The stenographer was busy. My tormentor needed proof of his effort.

I felt that my composure was becoming superficial. Inside, I started to feel a whirl of fear, uncertainty, despair and, above all, anger. My father had taught me that anger is one of the worst *midos*, but at this moment, I felt a relief in my anger. It gave me more incentive to fight. No, he wouldn't have it so easy with me. When he stopped after some weighty argument to hear my reaction, I asked him if he would give me more time to think it over. Of course, I hadn't the slightest intention of agreeing, but whatever would happen to me, let the *natchalnik* have it the hard way. His face registered triumph; he was sure I was giving in. He motioned to the sentry, and I was sent back to my cell.

There I could be myself again, but I couldn't sleep. My calm disappeared. My decision not to sign was firm. It was the alternative that drilled like a sharp screw deep into my mind and heart. I could easily believe I would not see my mother again before being imprisoned and sent away. It was a long-practiced method. Thousands disappeared in a similar way. I sat on the bench, feelings and thoughts in a wild race. I cried and prayed. Would I merit Hashem's pity for my mother's sake? Why was I doubting? I had promised to be strong. "Adhere to your *bitachon*," a voice inside me murmured. "Hold on, hold on."

The glare of the bulb was competing with the first, unsure rays of light stealing through the barred window. Little by little, the K.G.B.'s perversion of light had to surrender to the overpowering "Let there be light" of the Creator. So will it be, I said to myself. The light of the Creator will guide me in the darkness of human degradation.

I looked at the little window, and as it became lighter and lighter, my hope and strength rose. I heard the door opening, the changing of the milk and pita. After two days without food, I didn't feel hungry any more. I drank some of the water and returned to my seat on the bench.

The morning turned into day, the day into night. I still couldn't sleep. The screech of the lock and the sentry's voice telling me to come to the *natchalnik* didn't scare me so much now. In total isolation and stillness, even the barking of a dog is a welcome sound. It was two o'clock in the morning this time. The K.G.B. expected me to sign and get it over with— a short session.

When I entered the room, the set-up was the same as on the previous two nights, the K.G.B. head in his place at the desk, the other two on both sides. The sentry remained at the door. Without any preliminary talk, he took out the paper, turned it upside down and, holding the tip of his pen on the line where I was supposed to sign, motioned to my chair and waited. As I didn't stir, he assumed I wanted to read what I was signing first. He tried to be helpful.

"You want to read it yourself, or should I read it to you?" he asked.

"Neither," I said. "I will not sign, and I will not become an informer."

My declaration struck him like a thunderbolt. He jumped from his chair, and with the look of a hungry tiger teased with a slab of meat beyond his reach, gave a roar to the sentry, "Take her to the cellar!"

During Stalin's reign the K.G.B. cellars had a reputation of their own. I don't know if there were eyewitnesses to tell what happened there, because I doubt if anyone ever survived. The sentry stood ready, waiting for me to come to the door.

My mind exploded. I had to think quickly, on the spot. A fraction of a second could seal my fate. I turned, took a quick look at the distance between the desk and the door and decided to try. There was nothing to lose. As I neared the door I threw myself on the floor, hands and feet thrashing, my whole body convulsing violently, eyes almost closed. Through my slitted eyes I watched for the reaction. I had witnessed an epileptic seizure once, and I was sure I was copying it correctly. The only thing I couldn't reproduce was the foam around the mouth. It went unnoticed.

Thrashing continuously, I caught sight of the K.G.B. head going to the phone. He spoke quickly, replaced the receiver and sat back down at his desk. I didn't hear what he said because my thrashing blocked out his words, but I could see he was nervous. If it happened in the cellar it was perfectly acceptable, but a death in his office might carry an unpleasant aftertaste.

After about ten minutes, a short, middle-aged woman, carrying a black satchel came rushing in. I didn't stop thrashing. She sat down on the floor near me, took my pulse, raised my eyelids, opened her bag, took out a syringe, filled it with some liquid from a tiny bottle, pulled up my sleeve and injected it into my arm. For a moment, a wild thought passed through my mind. Maybe she had injected something lethal! My shaking now became more real than faked.

She looked around the room, turned to the K.G.B. head and asked if he'd allow her to transfer me to the couch. She wanted to make a closer examination.

"Don't move," she said. "We'll help you."

I suddenly realized that she had seen through my act and decided to play along with me.

The two assistants left the room, but the head interrogator was still at his desk. She asked for two blankets. The sentry brought them. She folded one, put it under my head and covered me with the other.

She held my hand as if checking my pulse again. I saw how she felt for me and how, in her limited way, she was trying to help. She put the stethoscope to my chest, asked about illnesses in the family, my health history and so on. I didn't stop shaking. I was in pain from the effort, but I decided to play it as long as possible. My answers through chattering teeth were barely audible. The doctor didn't need them. When she finished the examination, she gave me two pills, and talking to nobody in particular, she said that I must lie completely still and in four hours take another two pills. She knew that four hours of rest on a soft couch would do me no harm.

The *natchalnik* left the room together with the doctor. As he passed the sentry, he told him something which I didn't hear. The big light fixture was ablaze, and the sentry remained at the door. I tried not to fall asleep and to keep shaking all the time. I stole a look at my watch; it was almost four o'clock in the morning.

Sometime later, I heard someone talking quietly to the sentry. I didn't hear the question, but I heard the sentry's reply, "Still shaking."

Still shaking and still trapped.

Shortly before eight, the sentry told me to get up and take the other two pills, then he escorted me to my cell. The fresh pint of milk and the pita remained untouched. I wondered idly what the doctor had injected. Probably vitamins, as most likely were the pills. Regardless of the shortage of basic goods, vitamins were easily available.

I was sitting on the bench. I preferred to sit. Walking back and forth made me feel like a butterfly trapped between a double window, flying from one glass pane to the other, up and down, again and again, desperately looking for the smallest crack through which to escape. Sitting, although it was no less tiring, made me feel more assured. I was in possession of something, if only the narrow, cold bench beneath me.

What next? I asked myself. The same game twice was unthinkable. But what else? How long would my endurance hold up? How long would his patience restrain him? If not yesterday, surely it would be today. The K.G.B. basement seemed to be my inescapable destination.

Time became something unreal, elusive. I felt a fog envelop my head. It was swathed in a cloud of white cotton, which became bigger and bigger, like a huge ball of cotton candy; I myself became small and thin, like the stick that holds it.

When I woke up, the little window was dark gray. My watch had stopped. I had forgotten to wind it. It didn't matter anyway. Time had different dimensions in jail.

It took me a while to revive my stiffened limbs. How long had I been sleeping? I wondered. Probably the pills in the morning were sleeping pills, and I had been sleeping all day. The doctor knew the K.G.B. schedule.

The next drilling session started at one o'clock in the morning as usual; I could tell by the clock on the wall. It already felt like a routine procedure. The previous night's incident wasn't mentioned. He was angry, rude and, after two hours of spitting venom, infuriated. On hearing my only reaction, a firm refusal, he grabbed one of his pistols, ran over to the place where I was sitting, and when I jumped to my feet, sure that he was going to shoot me, he dug the barrel of the gun into my side and with wild force pushed me out of the room. In half a minute, I was back in my cell. My side hurt so much when I sat down that I stood the rest of the night leaning against the wall. Despite the pain, I felt a great relief. The slightest flick of his finger would have meant the end.

At one time during that day, I remember standing with my forehead resting against the wall, both hands raised, praying with my own words, with all my heart and soul, with all my being. I prayed in total forgetfulness of my surroundings. I was oblivious to the pain in my side, the thirst, the hunger, the tiredness, to the cell itself, to the K.G.B. head down the long hall. Everything disappeared. Time stopped. Every fiber of my soul and body was totally absorbed in prayer. I felt that a part of me was floating out of the cell, carried away on the wings of prayer to the very gates of Heaven.

When the door opened, I was sitting on the bench again.

It was ten o'clock in the evening. Unusual. Why so early?

"To the *natchalnik*," the sentry commanded.

I went, expecting the worst.

There were the three of them as usual. The head held a sheet of paper in his hand and, saying only one word, put it on the desk in front of me. "*Podpishy,*" he said. "Sign."

"I can only say what I have said the last four times. I will not sign."

"This you will sign," he said.

"What is this?"

"Read."

I read. It contained only three lines. "I obligate myself never, to anybody, under any circumstances, to disclose what took place here during the last five days."

"This I will sign." I put down the date and signed my name. He motioned to the sentry, and I was led outside the front door of the building. And although I did not feel bound by this promise extracted from me under extreme duress, I actually refrained from discussing my experiences with the K.G.B. in Poludieno until I left Russia.

CHAPTER 10

—■—

A Fugitive in Petropavlovsk

IT WAS A CLOUDY AND MOONLESS THURSDAY NIGHT. I ASKED the sentry the way to Tokushy. Surprisingly, he answered and even gave me some good advice, probably because of the milk and bread I had left him during my hunger strike.

"Go to the station and proceed alongside the tracks to your right," he said. "The road used by trucks and wagons leads through a forest, and in the darkness you may lose your way."

I thanked him and did as he advised.

I tried to walk alongside the tracks, but the ground was muddy and uneven. Between the rails will be easier, I thought, and I climbed up the embankment. It was easier, but every ten or fifteen minutes, a train behind me or in front of me forced me to climb down and wait until it passed. Despite not having eaten for days, I managed to walk the fourteen kilometers to Tokushy, although it did take me ten hours. I suppose I inherited my physical strength from my father and from my Grodno grandfather who could break a horseshoe with his bare hands.

When I knocked on the door of our little house, it was six o'clock in the morning. My mother was up and dressed, as if she were expecting me. Her control was remarkable. She showed no surprise or emotion. With her remarkable perception, my mother knew it wasn't the right time to talk; she would question me later. She hurried to give me a glass of milk and quietly said, "Go to sleep." I always admired my mother's usual perception, deep understanding and insightful evaluation of every situation. She never uttered an unnecessary word, but always said the right thing at the right time.

I went to bed and fell asleep immediately. The activity in the room—Etia with her two boys and Kreina with her family—was kept to a minimum so as not to disturb my sleep. When I awoke, I saw that they were making final preparations for *Shabbos*. It took me a while to realize where I was. The week spent at the K.G.B. headquarters seemed a wild nightmare. My whole body hurt. My side, where the *natchalnik* had stuck the gun barrel, felt sore to the touch. I felt very weak and hungry.

"I would like something to eat," I said to my mother.

She went to the big oven, pulled out the pot containing the *Shabbos* meal, put some in a bowl and gave me water to wash my hands. Still in a daze, I sat up and finished my meal in no time. Now I started to see things more clearly. I saw my mother, Etia, Kreina and her mother-in-law *bentch licht* over the single, glass-covered kerosene lamp which was placed for *Shabbos* on the corner shelf and turned down low. I saw the table covered with a white cloth. All were silent, not looking at each other or talking. I couldn't pinpoint what it was, but I felt a certain tension, an unease. I was too tired to think about it any longer, and I turned to the wall and fell asleep again. My mother allowed me to stay in her bed and used my bed on the trunk instead.

Usually, all of us were up early on *Shabbos* morning to prepare the room for the *minyan*. But this *Shabbos*, I woke up late and nobody came. I stayed in bed all day. The room, always a beehive of activity, was quiet and still. I got sympathetic looks from Etia and Kreina, but no one spoke.

When I came to the *artel* on Sunday morning and took my usual seat, however, the women and girls with whom I had worked so long and become friends avoided my eyes and wouldn't utter a word. I understood the reason. They were afraid. If I had been kept in K.G.B. headquarters for five days and released, it probably meant I had agreed to become an informer.

At home, the relationship normalized. The K.G.B. episode was never mentioned. Etia and I continued working in our garden late into the night for the second year, expecting the same results. Liba moved to Petropavlovsk with her daughter Freidele and son Lazar. Kreina and her family stayed with us.

My mother never asked me what had happened in Poludieno. She knew that as soon as I could, I would tell her myself. A few weeks later, I felt up to it.

Once the subject was broached, she told me how Etia, who was terrified of the K.G.B., had insisted on going to Poludieno to look for me, with no idea of what she would do should she find me; in her intensely impulsive way, she had felt compelled to do something, no matter what, and had actually walked the whole way to Poludieno to find me. In Poludieno, she consulted with friends of ours, who, of course, knew nothing about my being there. She even considered knocking on the doors of the K.G.B. building itself, but fortunately, she was dissuaded from that approach. She came home not having learned anything about my status or location. Not surprisingly, my mother had worried even more, but she had had *bitachon*.

Meanwhile, I became like an outcast among our own people. Whenever I happened to enter a room, the conversation would stop immediately and nervous glances would be exchanged by all present. I well understood their reaction. I knew the fear which pervaded Russia. But it hurt.

The Friday night and *Shabbos minyanim* were discontinued. People preferred to stay away from me.

Four weeks after I returned from Poludieno, on a Wednesday evening, Brodatch, Aaron David's son-in-law, appeared at our door. I was surprised because even he, a good friend, had curtailed his visits to us.

"I want to ask you something," he said to me, ignoring the puzzled looks of everyone in the room. He inclined his head indicating that I should come outside. It was after ten o'clock, but in the north, the summer days are very long, and at that late hour, it was still light enough to read outside.

"I was just walking in the street," Brodatch began, "and I was stopped by Vasiliev, the village chairman, who showed me this card and asked if I knew the person whose name is written on it. He said he'd never heard of such a person. Although the name on the card is yours, I replied that I also didn't know who it was, but if he let me have the card, I'd ask around. If I found the person, I'd deliver it."

The peculiarity of this conversation—Vasiliev and Brodatch

both knew that each of them knew me—didn't surprise me a bit. It only showed how serious the matter was. With trembling hands I took the card.

"Thursday, 25 June, ten o'clock in the morning," I read. "Dina Shapiro is to report to the police in Poludieno in order to be sent to a hard labor camp in Yakutia in the Arctic zone. Take along a change of clothing and bread." The Poludieno K.G.B. head had kept his promise.

"Can you imagine?" said Brodatch. "Vasiliev, whom we all considered a beast and an anti-Semite, should walk around Tokushy for three hours after closing his office in order to meet someone he could trust and who knows you, just so he could warn you?"

"So all his shouts and threats were just a cover up!" I said in wonder. "And how afraid I was of him!"

So insidious were the corrupting effects of the Soviet regime that in order to appear a devoted Communist one had to hide one's humanity and act a beast!

"You must run away and hide," said Brodatch. "The place to go is Petropavlovsk, to Masha. She'll find a place for you. Trains pass through our station every half hour or so. You must wait until it gets completely dark, and when a train stops, climb aboard between the cars. Remember to jump from the train as it slows down before it reaches Petropavlovsk. If you need money, I'll lend you a few hundred *rubles*."

I thanked him, but I didn't need the loan. He wished me luck and left.

I came into the house as if nothing had happened. To camouflage my nervousness, I took some yarn and started to knit. This was a familiar enough sight. My mother went to sleep, the others as well, but Etia was still up. After knitting a while, I put a hand to my cheek and started to complain of a toothache. The supposed pain increased by the minute, and my moaning woke my mother. I couldn't tell my mother I had to hide, but a sharp toothache was an understandable reason to go to Petropavlovsk. I was sure my mother suspected a more serious reason, and she also knew that without a permit, my travelling would be less than comfortable. Nonetheless, it wasn't in her nature to despair and become hysterical. Her calm and strength sustained me.

Etia went outside and motioned to me to follow. I didn't want to tell my mother and cause her a distressing night. Someone ought to know, I thought, and so I told Etia the whole story. We decided that in the morning she would tell my mother that it was appendicitis that had forced me to go to town and see a doctor. I was sure there would be inquiries from the police. My mother would give them the same answer, that I was hospitalized in Petropavlovsk with appendicitis. With their visits, everything would become quite clear to my mother and everyone else, but until then, not one word was to be said about it to anyone.

I left the house after midnight, empty-handed. I took only a few hundred *rubles* tied in a handkerchief and secured with a safety pin inside my dress. Luckily, it was a moonless night. I waited for a train at a distance from the station building, outside the perimeter of light from the two pole lamps.

The war was still in full swing, and dozens of trains carrying military equipment and soldiers went through Tokushy and Petropavlovsk every week on the way from the Far East to the European front. But to board a train carrying soldiers was too risky, since every car had a guard. Passenger trains to Petropavlovsk were also out of the question, since they passed our station only twice a day, both times in full daylight. The only possibility was a freight train.

My heartbeat matched the click-clack of the rolling wheels, as I stood in the shadows waiting for a freight train. The freight was usually armaments, and although they didn't have guards on every car, getting caught on such a train meant a bullet on the spot. But I had no choice. I recognized the next freight train as soon as the hissing, smoke-and-steam-enveloped locomotive passed. The train was long, a combination of closed boxcars and open platforms covered with khaki canvas, showing the contours of its lethal cargo.

Tokushy was a big station, and every passing train stopped for at least a few minutes. I chose a place between two boxcars, as there was less exposure there. My railroad training proved to be helpful now. Bending low, I ran from my shadowed hiding place to the train, grabbed a coupling pin with both hands, put one foot on the chain which connected the plates of the two boxcars and pulled myself up. Just in time, I stepped with both feet on the pin and caught a protruding rod from the side of the car when the train started moving.

The pins were round and slippery, the train was shaking, and the rusty piece of iron, which I held tightly by turning slightly sideways, rubbed my hands like a file. My head and side were plastered to the wall of the car, and all my attention was on my feet. I was afraid to close my eyes, but I couldn't keep them open either. Accustomed to the darkness now, the sight of the flitting landscape—trees and shadows, the gravel, rails and the view all around—made my head whirl like a propeller.

When will the train stop? I thought. When will this hell end? But I didn't dare wait for the train to stop. What had Brodatch said? That I should jump when the train slowed down before it reached the station. Meanwhile, it just sped along. A blur. All my muscles were as tightly strung as a wire, numbed by the tension and effort to keep my balance and by the whirlwind on both sides of the train and around me between the cars. Then a burst of sparks, steam and smoke from a train going in the opposite direction on the next track almost swept me to the ground and under the wheels. It was good that I was wearing a dark dress; it made me invisible.

The train, like myself, was a fugitive, I from the K.G.B., the train from the night. The darkness dissipated, and through the foggy, pre-dawn grayness, I could see that Petropavlovsk was close by. I prepared to jump at the first indication of the train slowing its tempo. From afar, I noticed the contours of buildings. Instinctively, I felt that the instant I let go of the rod I had to jump, otherwise I'd lose my balance and fall between the cars. Another kilometer rolled by before I took the plunge. The moment came. With eyes closed, I found myself rolling down the embankment, the grinding rumble fading away overhead. The train passed. I was still lying on the ground, waiting for some pain or sign of injury, and at the same time watching the disappearing train with great relief. No one had seen me.

The ground felt damp and cold. I stood up, feeling my legs, sides, arms. Thank Heaven, not a scratch. I had put my trust in Hashem and was rewarded with a miracle.

The day grew brighter, and I started into town. I knew Masha's address; I had stayed there a few times while looking for information about my father. She and her two young daughters were refugees from Kharkov in the Ukraine. Like many other Soviet Jews, they had fled from the Germans. Her husband was in the army, and to supplement her meager pension, she shared her two-room apartment with short term boarders. She provided no food for her boarders, of course;

food was too scarce. The boarders had to be trustworthy people, recommended by friends. Brodatch was a frequent guest, as his business often took him to Petropavlovsk. Ravtzov had recommended him to Masha, and he had recommended me. After two hours, I reached her apartment, covered with dust and soot. I told her I had to hide for a while.

"Not in my apartment," she insisted. "I don't want to endanger myself and my children. I'll give you a note for a woman I know who lives on the outskirts, on the other end of town. She can be trusted." She quickly scribbled a few words on a piece of old newspaper and told me the address which I had to memorize, so there would be no written evidence in case I was caught. She was visibly eager to get rid of me, but she offered me just a glass of water before I left.

Tired, dirty and hungry, I started my first day as a fugitive. Petropavlovsk is a big, dilapidated Siberian town, and after another two hours of walking around and asking directions from elderly *babushkas*, I finally reached the woman's home. It was a lot like a peasant's hut, with a fenced vegetable garden and an attached barn.

I came into the yard and knocked on the door. A loud bark was the first answer. Next, a tall, slender woman, shoving away a big black dog, stepped outside. I gave her the note. She read it, nodded and led me inside. In the note, Masha had written only that she was sending a boarder. The rest of my story I had to repeat myself. No details, of course. For a good price, she provided her boarders with food also, like bread, milk, vegetables and eggs.

"At the moment, my boarders are away, so you can wash up and eat," she told me. "But you cannot stay in the house. Nobody should see you. I'll make you a place in the barn. You can stay there as long as you have to. With food, it will cost you a hundred *rubles* a day."

"I will eat only bread, milk and vegetables," I said. "Nothing cooked."

"It makes no difference," she answered. "I'm taking a chance hiding you."

I agreed to her conditions. After three days, she doubled the price. Again, I agreed.

Refreshed from the wash and the meal, I followed my landlady to see the barn. My new roommates were a big black cow with white spots and a number of chickens, including a rooster. Spiders, beetles, flies and all kinds of creeping creatures were frequent but temporary visitors. The cow's stall occupied the space to the right of the door. Above, two rods, fastened across the width of the barn wall to wall, served as a perch for the chickens. On the left side in the near corner was a stack of hay. The far corner was to be my domain.

After sweeping it clean, the woman brought in an old barn door from a shed nearby and jammed it tightly between the two corner walls, forming a triangle. Behind this partition, she put a straw-filled mattress covered with a thick homespun sheet, and a small stool. Then she brought in a small pillow and another sheet as a cover. That was it. My room was ready. To get in or out, I had to climb over the partition. I preferred the exercise to being trampled by the cow's hooves in case she ever decided to leave her stall and take a walk around the barn, although the woman assured me this wouldn't happen. During the day, the barn was empty. The cow was out in the field to pasture, and the chickens were all over the yard.

I thanked the woman and climbed in. The moment my head touched the pillow, benevolent sleep wiped out the barn, the train, the K.G.B., the dog and the cow—my whole current world.

A cacophony of mooing, barking and squawking brought me right back to reality. I opened my eyes, and in the semi-darkness of the barn, from my place on the straw mattress behind the partition, my first sight was of a fluttering of gray, black and white wings and a tangle of yellow feet and claws positioning themselves on the perch under the barn ceiling. I was too tired to sit up. From the sounds, I knew exactly what was going on. I heard the cow charging through the door, rustling to a stop in the hay and then lapping the water the woman had prepared for her in a big, deep, wooden basin. Soon after, I heard the measured sound of the first streams of milk hitting the tin pail, becoming duller as the pail filled. I heard the door of the house close and open again.

I was sitting on the little stool, my feet on the mattress, when the woman came to my corner.

"I brought you milk and bread," she said. "Do you want anything else? My boarders are coming any minute, and I don't want them to see that I'm taking food to the barn."

"Just bring me a pail with water, a cup and a towel please. Are you sure the cow won't come here? I'm afraid of her horns."

"I tied her up to a hook," she reassured me. "She can't reach you."

She brought what I asked, as well as an additional blanket, one of the large, heavy wraps the Siberian women used for everything. I heard her bolting the door from the outside. Soon, footsteps, voices, the opening and closing of the door to the house and the guard dog's barking indicated the presence of her boarders.

The bread she had brought me, a big chunk, was wrapped

in a towel smelling of fresh air and sun. The milk was strained and still warm in a liter jug three-quarters full. It was a meal fit for a king. (Interestingly, when she raised the rent three days later, the food portions diminished in reverse proportion.) I ate slowly, enjoying every bite. It had been a long time since I had experienced such calm and serenity. The immediate past and future were completely blocked out. All I had or cared about were the here and now. I liked my corner, I liked the cow, and I liked the chickens. Why can't cows and chickens rule the nations of the world? I asked myself. How much happier and safer people would be!

The swishing sound of the cow's tail fending off the creeping and flying insects brought me back to my most immediate reality. As long as she only fanned herself, it didn't bother me. It was the thought that maybe she'd decide to extend her hospitality by flapping her tail in my direction that worried me for a moment. Now that my eyes had adjusted to the semi-darkness, I took a closer look. Seeing the distance that separated my corner from the cow, I finished my supper relaxed and unperturbed.

The night set in. Every place has its own noises. Here it was the occasional twitter of a sleeping chicken, the cow chewing her cud, a barely audible swish in the hay, probably from a field mouse, the zoom of a mosquito, and probably many more sounds which the human ear is not equipped to detect. The air was a cloud of odors. The delicious, strong smell of freshly cut hay and the barely detectable currents of crisp, unpolluted air coming through the slits between the boards of the barn wall contrasted with the heavy, steamy odors of the cow, the manure and the chicken droppings.

I couldn't fall asleep for a while, not because I had been sleeping all afternoon, but because the creeping insects disturbed me. Ever since I was a child, when playmates had once dropped a beetle down my dress and responded to my cries with delighted shrieks, I felt a revulsion for anything that crawls. It seemed, though, that half a day's rest really wasn't enough. Overwhelmed with fatigue, my anxiety gave way, and I fell asleep.

In a household with domestic animals and birds, the day starts early. Most zealous of all is the rooster. Flapping his wings and crowing his unique cock-a-doodle-doo, every morning he races the rising sun. In no time after his alarm, the activity in the barn got hectic. The cowherd came early to collect his charges. In Petropavlovsk, a town of about one hundred thousand inhabitants, most of the families, excluding refugees, kept a cow. The milking had to be done quickly and the cow led to the gate. The chickens were again let out into the yard, and the now empty barn was all mine.

My breakfasts were late, after everyone left, and my suppers early, before they all came back. During the day, some wanderer would occasionally stop by, so my movements were restricted, and I seldom left my corner. But it was all fine with me. My landlady provided adequately for my needs, and there was nothing I wanted to do elsewhere.

On Sunday, a very welcome guest appeared in the barn. It was Brodatch. Over one arm he had my light brown jacket and a change of clothing; it was safer that way, since a wrapped package could arouse suspicion. He also brought some money as a loan, which I gave to the woman for a week's advance, and another precious item, a stub of pencil and a piece of paper. My mother already knew the truth, Brodatch told me. Three days in a row—Thursday, Friday and Saturday—policemen from Poludieno had come to look for me, and not just for my staying away from work without leave.

I wrote a brief note, which Brodatch delivered to my mother the next day. A letter exchange between my mother and me began. The letters consisted of only two or three words so as not to be incriminating. We just wanted to see each other's handwriting. This became a weekly routine.

In between my mother's weekly letters, my life was one long stretch of boredom and monotony, broken by an occasional minor disaster. One night I awoke to find myself soaked, together with my pillow and mattress. An unusually stormy rain had sent torrents of water through the slits in the barn walls at my corner. The ground became a mud pool. The only thing I could do was to put everything over the top of the enclosure and sit on my stool until the rain and the night were over.

The instinct of self-preservation is probably the strongest element in human nature. The most important difference between my barn corner and the Poludieno jail cell was the peace and security, but as far as isolation went, they had quite a lot in common. In order to save my sanity, I instinctively transported myself to another world, another time. What is time anyway? Is it only a sum total of minutes, days or years? Or is it the intensity of events? Is it the passage from one second to the next, or the passage from one event to another?

Time and thought. Both are substantial and real, both elusive and indefinable. Can the speed of thought be measured? Its direction determined? Is the present moment real, or the remembrance of it?

CHAPTER 11

■

Glimpses from the Past

THE SPINNING DIAL OF MY MEMORIES SCANNED THE golden years of my childhood and settled on Grodno. Every *Rosh Chodesh*, my father, Uncle Yaakov and Uncle Shmuel from Suvalki visited their parents in Grodno. The closeness of the brothers and sisters to their parents and to each other was unmatched. Before I started school, my father often took me along on these visits, but my uncles seldom brought their children. My grandmother was ill, and they didn't want to disturb her with too much commotion. For me, those were the most cherished days I can remember. We left our bags in Aunt Julia's or Aunt Tania's apartment, which was nearby, situated on a square block of park-like grounds which had been my grandfather's parents' property.

I remember the excitement I felt before entering my

grandparents' house. I also remember the instructions Aunt Julia used to give me. Don't make any noise, don't run around and don't touch anything. Even my father and uncles, who had grown up in this house, would enter it with respect. A live-in, middle-aged couple with two teenage children took care of the household and all my grandparents' needs.

I remembered the big, square foyer and the very long, narrow dining room. The drapes were always drawn, which made the half-lit room gloomy. In the foyer were several doors, but as I was told not to roam, I never saw what was behind them. I knew that one door led to my grandfather's room, because when we entered he used to come out and greet his sons with a handshake. This was one of the rare occasions when he smiled. He also smiled at me and called me "little kitten." He took my father and uncles to his room, but I never went there. Instead, I was led through the long dining room to an even darker salon, and from there through another foyer to my grandmother's room.

It was like the bright sun suddenly appearing among dark clouds. I don't remember how the dining room and living room were furnished, but I recall every detail of my grandmother's room. It was an echo of the grandeur of her younger years. The whole house was still furnished with the luxury her parents had provided for her when she married, lacking only the things she had given to her children.

But it wasn't the furnishings that made the room bright; it was my grandmother herself. Only in her room was the regality of her presence felt, because she herself was there. Each time I saw her, I thought this must be what an angel looks like. She was very weak. I never saw her walk or even stand. In the short time I was allowed to spend with her, she always sat on a high-backed wing chair, upholstered in petit point with a matching stool under her feet. On a small, beautifully carved table nearby was a *siddur* with a frayed cover, testimony to frequent use. In a corner was a four-poster brass bed, each post so thick and elaborate it could stand as a decoration by itself. The bed was unmade, because a few times a day she was carried from the chair to the bed for a rest. On the floor was a worn but still beautiful antique rug, and against one wall was a big bureau with many delicate objects on it which, remembering Aunt Julia's warnings, I never dared to touch.

My grandmother was petite and delicate, with a sweet, ethereal smile which never left her face. When I entered her room I didn't run, although I wanted to, but slowly walked to her chair, put my head on her lap and kissed her hand. I felt her trembling hand caress my hair. Had I been allowed, I could have remained for hours just standing near her. My grandmother also called me "little kitten."

After spending some time with my grandfather, my father and the uncles would come to see their mother. Though there were several chairs in the room, they never sat down. They would stand in a semicircle in front of her chair and bend to hear her words spoken in a low, soft voice. The reverence, respect and love they had for her filled the room with sunshine.

Her children admired her greatly for her willingness to forego the trappings of high society she had known in her parents' home in order to have a husband who was a *talmid chacham*, dedicated entirely to Torah. Having been raised as an only child, surrounded by extreme luxury, living on a silver cloud, she raised her children in a strict and decisive manner, imbuing them with the highest values and ethics of *Yiddishkeit*, with *midos tovos* and adherence to *mitzvos*.

She bore nine children. Three passed away in infancy. Her oldest daughter died during childbirth at the age of twenty-one. The tragedy broke my grandmother's heart. Her health started to fail and brought her to the condition in which I saw her, sitting in her beloved chair. Of course, at that time I didn't know all of this. Years later, Aunt Julia told me the story of my grandmother's life.

Meanwhile, each visit to Grodno was a holiday. When she was weaker, my father and uncles would carefully keep their visits to their mother short, only a few minutes, so as not to strain her. But when she felt a little stronger, my grandfather would join them, and then they would spend a longer time together, reminiscing about their grandfathers' and great-grandfathers' greatness in Torah learning and good deeds.

My grandmother, always smiling, would remark, "My children, it is clear that you can be proud of your grandfathers, but my wish is that, by your righteous life and good deeds, your grandfathers should be proud of you."

"Julia, can you show me the album with Grandmother's pictures?" It was a long overdue promise. I called all my aunts and uncles by first name only. The only exceptions were *Tiotia* (Aunt in Russian) Gittel and *Diadia* (Uncle) Yaakov. Aunt Gittel was always *Tiotia* to me, even in my letters to her from Siberia.

Julia, the serious, practical, logical, smart, strong-minded "man with two heads," as she was called by the family, was extremely sensitive and sentimental about everything that concerned my grandmother and her family. Her younger sister Toby Esther, whom we called Tania, was a complete contrast to her in looks and disposition. Soft-spoken and quiet, she was more concerned with the present than with the past. She wasn't interested in the albums. From all her mother's treasures, she chose the collection of knick-knacks. Every room in her apartment contained little corner shelves, display cabinets and vitrines filled with carved ivory, mother-of-pearl, amber and rare porcelain. She also had the paintings that had first adorned my grandmother's room. Her apartment looked like a small museum.

Aunt Julia had no interest in decoration. Her seven-room apartment, filled with big, heavy furniture, had a formal, masculine atmosphere. She did have one decorative item from her mother–a corner etagere of rare, intricate, filigree-like work in solid silver. On the top shelf stood the *Shabbos* candelabra; the three lower shelves were empty. It was beautiful on its own, without anything obstructing the lacy design.

I was about six years old the first time Aunt Julia took the two heavy, gold-embossed, leather-bound albums out of her bedroom closet and put them on her dining room table; except for Aunt Julia, nobody on either side of the family was a photograph enthusiast, so she had a monopoly. It was the first time I saw pictures of my grandmother as a young girl. Her photograph was inserted on the first page of the album.

The impression it made on me then, though I was unaware of it at the time, revealed itself decades later in two things that even today make me sad–the sight of wilted flowers and the sight of photographs of people when they were young and then of the same people fifty years later.

I had just come from my grandmother's house. She was sweet and smiling as always. Her hands shook, her face had deep wrinkles, and she was dependent on someone's help to put her to bed or in the chair. This was my grandmother as I knew and loved her. But now I was looking at the picture in the album of a stunningly beautiful young girl, a diamond tiara supporting a high pompadour which fell in long banana curls to her shoulders and back. Under her high ruffled collar she wore a diamond necklace, wide as a bib. She stood full height, with one hand resting on the back of a chair. A ring with a huge stone seemed to cover half of her small hand.

"This is a picture of your grandmother when she became engaged to your grandfather," Julia told me.

I envisioned my grandfather in his deep carpet slippers, in his dark brown *chalat* (robe) tied with a belt, which emphasized his bent back; I saw his serious face, his sharp look.

"Your grandfather was also young, only one year older than Grandmother." Aunt Julia, like her father, could answer questions before they were asked.

"Is there a picture of Zeide like this?"

"No. Your grandfather never let himself be photographed," Julia told me. "He was against photographs."

"I want to see more pictures of Grandmother," I declared.

"After she married, there were no more pictures. This album contains photographs of your grandmother's family, and also many of her as a child and growing up, but we'll look at them another time." She saw how shaken I was, and decided I was too young to grasp the reality of life, that a beautiful young girl can turn into a sick, wrinkled and helpless old woman.

Likewise, my Lida Zeide had no photographs of himself, except a few taken in his later years, on his obligatory Polish passports. My mother and father shared the same indifference to taking pictures. There were no photographs of me until the age of eight. Then one day, my mother told me to dress up nicely, and we went to Mr. Glauberman's, the best photo studio in town. I was very excited looking at myself in my white velvet dress, hair parted in the middle with two long dark braids reaching almost to my knees. Since I had started school, my father seldom took me on the monthly visits to Grodno, and my grandmother had asked for a picture.

The last time I saw her, she wasn't sitting in her chair, she was in bed. She always gave me little presents from her chest, treasures such as a carved ivory fan in a silver frame or a miniature amber inkwell in the form of a carved flower. I treasured them all, but the one dearest to me was the little silver change purse which she gave me when I saw her for the last time. It was in her bureau drawer, and she told me to take it out. It was the same purse that, years later, lay together with all our other silver items, mostly presents to my parents from my grandparents, on the floor of the N.K.V.D. office in Lida.

The same angelic smile my grandmother always wore didn't leave her face at the moment of her death. All her children were at her bedside. Her last words were, "Do not cry. I am dying the happiest mother in the world, knowing that I'm leaving children such as you."

After my grandmother passed away, my father and uncles continued the monthly visits. When they coincided with a day off from school, I would go along, but it was not the same. The house seemed even darker and sadder. It was probably so for my grandfather, as well. From then on, I don't remember him ever smiling. He seldom left the house, immersing himself totally in learning Torah, which he had been doing all his life anyway. Among the visitors, besides the family, was the famous *gaon* and *rosh yeshivah* Rabbi Shimon Shkop, who until the end of Grandfather's life used to come every *Shabbos* afternoon to discuss Torah matters.

A few years passed, and one cold February evening, Uncle

Asher, Julia's husband, phoned us. Early the next morning, my father and Uncle Yaakov took their *talleisim* and *tefillin* and went to Grodno. My grandfather had passed away.

A year later, my father came home from the office carrying a flat, wrapped package. It contained my grandmother's picture, a copy of the one I had seen on the first page Aunt Julia's album.

"I have to go to Warsaw tomorrow, and I want to give it to a good photographer to make five enlargements, one for each of her children," my father said. My father also arranged to have all of them framed.

When the picture arrived, a huge portrait in a wide, gilded frame, it was hung above the piano, in the best view from the entrance.

"Why did you hang up a portrait of a princess?" one of my father's acquaintances asked on a visit to us.

"She was more than a princess," my father replied. "She was my mother."

"Why did you hang up a portrait of a queen?" asked my friends when they first saw it.

"She was more than a queen," I replied. "She was my grandmother."

CHAPTER 12

■

The Power of Words

THE REMINISCENCES WERE FLASHING, OVERLAPPING each other, and a detail from a few years later appeared on the screen. I was grown then and refurnishing my room shortly before the war. I had ordered a bureau and a wardrobe closet from a Polish master craftsman to my own specifications and design. The wood I chose was the most expensive, blond wood with natural black specks. The carpenter was a perfectionist and it took a long time, but when he delivered it, it was even better than I had expected. Admiring the pieces standing in my room, I asked the carpenter what I should pay him. He mentioned an exorbitant price.

"*Tak drogo?*" I exclaimed, caught by surprise. "So expensive?"

My father heard me from the other room. He called me over and said, "Did you ask him what it would cost when you ordered it?"

"No, I didn't," I confessed.

"Then how can you know it's too much? If you don't agree on a price before ordering, you have to pay whatever he asks. Only he himself can appraise his work."

It was a lesson for me in justice and in dealing with people for all the years to come.

My father was also very careful not to throw words around. He didn't make empty promises. Maybe and probably didn't exist in his vocabulary. "I will try," he would say. And in such cases he did try, and very hard. "I will do my best," he would sometimes say, but not as empty words spoken now, forgotten later. He did his best until he got results.

He was extremely careful not to hurt anyone's feelings, but on the other hand he was not generous with undeserved compliments. *Chanifah*, flattery, was one of his taboos. The same caution he used in performing business transactions, he applied in his speech. To mislead someone with a word or to evoke someone's trust by deception was *gneivah*, theft. Guarding his speech was one of his strongest principles. The following event illustrates the extent to which he practiced it.

My hearty appetite was cute when I was small, but in my teens it caused me anguish. Diets were short-lived. During the year, I exercised irregularly. Each summer, my parents and I would go to a resort place, my mother for mineral baths, my father for a vacation, and I for exercise programs of all kinds. The resort I liked most were the cascades in Druskieniki, the only resort place in eastern Poland. The resort was between Bialystok and Grodno in a scenic location along the Niemen

River, which formed a natural border between Poland and Lithuania.

The cascades were man-made waterfalls in an enclosed section of the Niemen River. The pools were built with walls for privacy and with railings along the sides for safety. The dams were of different heights and so was the strength of the falling water. There were separate hours for men and women, and attendants were always present to guard against accidents.

Fifteen minutes daily under a constant pounding of hundreds of cubic meters of water did take off a few kilos, which I compensated for, however, by a ravenous appetite.

In Krinitza and Truskavietz, resorts in southwestern Poland near the Carpathian mountains, there were enclosed solariums with swimming pools and all kinds of exercise equipment. It was an expensive program, paid for a month in advance and lasting four hours, five days a week. I was good at all the exercises except swimming. I could never learn to swim. But all that work was to no avail. After the summer was over and the home cooking was too tempting again, the traitorous pounds found their way back.

"Bicycle riding would be good exercise," someone suggested.

There were no stationary bicycles at that time, and obtaining a bicycle became an obsession.

"I'll buy you whatever you want, but not a bicycle," my father said after repeated pleas.

I had had a tricycle when I was six or seven years old, but at fifteen? Who ever heard of such a thing? I continued to plead.

"You know what," my father finally said, half-joking, "if you win the lottery, you can buy one yourself."

For years, my father and Uncle Yaakov had been buying lottery tickets, but they had never won. Julia's husband Asher, in Grodno, had a license to sell government lottery tickets— a big privilege—and he used to mail a few tickets to my father twice a year, when the drawings took place.

"Papa, is it a promise?" I asked.

"If you win," my father said, smiling.

Impatiently, I waited for the first day off from school and asked my parents if I could go to Grodno. I visited my relatives there often, so no objections were made. I took the early bus in order to be able to return the same day. In Grodno, I went straight to my Uncle Asher's office. He was surprised to see me and even more surprised when I told him I wanted to buy a lottery ticket.

"I sent your father the lottery tickets two months ago," he said.

"I want to buy one for myself," I declared. "But it has to be a secret."

My uncle laughed, took out a packet of tickets and said, "Pull one out."

I closed my eyes, fingered the tickets and, as if in a trance, tried to find the right one.

"What a long time it takes you to pick!" he exclaimed. "I sell ten thousand tickets each drawing; if they all picked like you it would take me ten years to sell them." He laughed at me as I hesitantly pulled one out. "Do you want a whole or a quarter?"

"How much is a whole?"

"Fifty *zlotys*."

"I'll take a quarter." I didn't want to press my luck. "But it's a secret."

"I can't promise to keep it a secret if you win," my uncle

answered, still laughing.

Whenever I remember my Grodno uncles, I always remember them laughing. Uncle Asher was a delightfully happy man, and when Aunt Tania's husband Uncle Moishe came for a visit, he made us laugh to tears. He was a jolly, happy-go-lucky person who thrived on practical jokes, sometimes, for example, sending my Uncle Yaakov a registered, express letter (which could only cause concern) containing only one word, "Smile!"

My business finished, I had just enough time to run to see my grandfather, my aunts and my great-aunt Golda Leah. She was the wife of my grandfather's youngest brother Binyamin. She had no children, and I was her beloved grandniece. I called her Golden Leah.

Back home, I had a late supper and did my homework. For the next few months, I followed my usual routine.

After dinner, my father always had a few glasses of tea. I was usually in my room at that time.

"Look, Eber," I heard Uncle Yaakov say one day. "I found this telegram from Asher in the office saying that one of our numbers won two thousand *zlotys*. I checked, but it's not one of our numbers. He probably made a mistake."

"It's mine! It must be mine! I won!" I jumped into the room, wild with excitement.

My parents and uncle looked at me. "How? When? When did you buy a ticket?"

"Papa, do you remember when I asked you for a bicycle, you said that if I'd win the lottery I could have one. The last time I went to Grodno, I bought a quarter."

It turned out that the whole ticket was worth two thousand, and that one of Uncle Asher's employees had written the wrong amount on the telegram.

"Yes," my father said after a long pause. "I do remember, and I will keep my word. It is not a coincidence. It is surely meant to teach us all a lesson about how careful we have to be with words and promises. A word, before you say it, is your slave. After you say it, you become its slave."

A few days later, a money order for four hundred *zlotys* arrived in my name. My quarter of a ticket had won five hundred, but twenty percent was deducted by the government for taxes and the agent's commission. I asked my father to exchange it for cash and to take off forty *zlotys* for *tzeddakah*, according to the laws of *maaser*.

With three hundred and sixty *zlotys* in my pocket, and my father's cautious and conditional approval, I went to Mr. Goldwasser's sports and bicycle store.

"I have three ladies' bicycles," he said. "Polish, Italian and British."

"Which is the best?" I asked.

"The British, but it is the most expensive. The Polish is two hundred *zlotys*, the Italian is two hundred and eighty, and the British is . . ." I held my breath as he paused dramatically, ". . . three hundred and sixty."

The bicycles hung on chains suspended from the ceiling, and with a long stick, he pointed to the special advantages of the British model over the other two.

"I'll take the British," I said.

He told his helper to take it down. It was really a beauty. The handles and frame were shiny nickel, the rear wheel was covered with a multicolored net, and on the center upright bar was a bell.

"I guarantee it is the best there is," he reassured me. "And any time you need adjustments or . . ." I gave him the money and didn't even hear the rest of his assurances.

It was dark when I brought it home, and a drizzle covered the shiny nickel with a net of tiny, pearly dots. Off the porch was a big, empty room with a roll-up roof used only once a year for a *sukkah*. I put the bicycle there.

I couldn't explain what it was. I had gotten what I wanted and in a most unusual way, but still I had an uneasy feeling. During supper, I couldn't hide my guilty look from my father. He was bound by his word, but in a way I had imposed it on him. The bicycle stayed in the *sukkah* for a few weeks until I was ready to start. I had to have a special dress made from material heavy enough not to flutter in the wind and long enough to cover my legs to the ankle. I chose a tan colored, denim-like material, took it to the dressmaker and told her what I wanted, not revealing its purpose.

"What will you do with such a dress?" she asked.

"Please make it just like that," I insisted.

But the dressmaker was not content to make it "just like that," and she did make it more attractive by adding brown leather buttons and a brown belt. When it was ready, I sewed a hook and eye at the hemline in front and in back to make it more secure.

The main conditions my father requested were that I never ride in the direction of town, and not at all on market days, and that I be very careful when crossing the railroad tracks.

The road to Vilna passed alongside our property. The traffic in those days was minimal. Twice a day, a bus to and from Vilna passed, aside from an occasional truck or a peasant's wagon. The road was smooth and even. On both sides, for about two kilometers, were rows of wooden houses set back from the road with front gardens, inhabited mostly by our workers and some poor Jewish families. I never ventured further, but often, I went back and forth several times to the end of the houses.

The desired miracle didn't occur, but it was good and healthy exercise and it gave me a lot of pleasure. And there was rarely a ride on which I did not contemplate the importance and power of words.

My memory dial turned back, and I was five years old again.

"Mama, I want to *daven* like you do in a big *siddur* with many, many words," I said to my mother one morning.

She was sitting at the dining room table, eyes closed, swaying slightly back and forth, deeply engrossed in a *tefillah* which she recited by heart. When she finished, my mother looked at me with surprise and smiled. It was the first time in all of my five and a half years that I had expressed a wish to learn to pray.

By then I knew *Modeh Ani*, all the *berachos* on food, the first two *berachos* of *bentching* and the first *parshah* of *Krias Shema*, all by heart, but these were achieved with my mother's endless patience and effort.

"If you will sit still for ten minutes, we can start the *alef-beis* right after breakfast," my mother said.

After breakfast, I ran to the couch, snuggled comfortably in my beloved corner and looked on with enthusiasm as my mother opened the cover of the big *siddur*. On the first page were the mysterious letters of the *alef-beis*. It was so cozy to sit near my mother and repeat each letter again and again. She constantly moved her index finger back and forth to see if I remembered the *alef* after learning through *daled*. My mother was surprised that after thirty minutes I was still sitting quietly.

The following year, I was very proud to stand each morning near my mother and recite the *Shemoneh Esrei*. At the end, watching her closely, I tried to bow as she did, take the three steps backward, bow and kiss the *siddur*.

My mother, by nature, never taught me by lecturing or explaining why I had to do things. She let me learn for myself about social and economic differences among people and the importance of *tzeddakah* by giving me neatly wrapped packages to deliver to needy families.

As a very young child, when I had brought the *Shabbos* packages to the potter, I was sure they lived in their little house because they liked it. Most of my childhood friends were from comfortable, middle class families. The only poor people I encountered were those who came to our house asking for help or those I met in the street.

But when I was twelve or thirteen years old, my eyes opened, and I had a better understanding of what life was like for others. Once, my mother handed me a package and told me to take it to the people whose name and address were written on it. I found the place and entered a crowded and untidy room. A number of small children were sitting on the platform of a Russian-style oven without any shoes. I recognized the woman, because I had seen her at our house a few times. After that, the trips with the packages became a weekly routine.

Another place my mother sent me with packages was to a widow with an eighteen-year-old daughter. They were from another town and had no family in Lida. The girl did beautiful hand-embroidery, and her earnings were their only source of income. Then tragedy struck. The girl contracted tuberculosis and was unable to work. I saw the mother come to us a few times, a fine and gentle woman, always departing with a sad smile. I knew my mother had helped her.

Every Thursday afternoon, regardless of the weather, I took a large bundle to their end of town, a poor neighborhood where they lived in a tiny, spotless attic. This went on for a long time. And then a miracle happened. The girl recovered completely and married a fine boy who was a good provider.

I realized that I had benefitted from delivering these packages as much as the recipients had, if not more. My mother could have given them money to buy whatever they needed, which would have been much simpler. But this was her way of teaching me about poverty and human suffering and, of course, about the importance of *tzeddakah*.

I learned another powerful lesson when I was ten, on one of Uncle Shmuel's visits. We were drinking tea after dinner, Russian style, and were engaged in lively conversation. Not wanting to be left out, I caught a moment of quiet and repeated something I had seen at a friend's house, where I had visited earlier.

My few words caused quite a stir at the table. My mother gave me a sharp look, Uncle Shmuel moved in his chair, raised the teaspoon he held in his hand and seemed ready to say something. But my father, his color rising, more agitated and angry than I had ever seen before or after, stood up and leaned over in my direction.

"Don't you know that *lashon hora* is one of the worst sins?" he asked in a strict voice. "Talking about what is happening in other people's houses, what other people eat or say or do is one of the worst kinds of *lashon hora*. It is even worse than a bullet. A bullet can only go so far. *Lashon hora* can kill a person thousands of miles away. I don't want to hear any talk about anyone ever again."

My father sat down, and Uncle Shmuel's voice broke the silence. His question was directed at me.

"Tell me, what is the difference between a smart person and a stupid one?" As I remained silent, he gave the answer himself. "A smart person knows what he says, and a stupid one says what he knows."

I understood what he meant. Even after so many years, having lived through so many events, my uncle's words and my father's severe reprimand are still burned into my memory.

My mother exemplified these teachings. She hosted many meetings of the various charitable organizations in which she was active. When tea was served after finishing the business at hand, my mother gently reminded the ladies in attendance that any topic was welcome except talk about people and their doings.

I couldn't control my memory. Picture after picture raced through my mind. One moment I saw myself at the age of fifteen, then a clear image flashed of an event that had occurred when I was five or six. The scenes were constantly shifting back and forth. The passage of time lost its significance. I lived again on the other side of the rainbow. If only I were there, I thought. This is just a nightmare, a bad dream. Soon I'll wake up and be home again.

CHAPTER 13

■

Summer Breezes

NOT ONLY INDIVIDUALS FROM VARIOUS SOCIAL AND intellectual levels were attracted to my father, but children and toddlers, led by their natural instincts, were drawn to him like a magnet.

One summer, after a very hectic period, my father felt he needed a quiet place for a few weeks of rest. Novoyelnia, the resort where my Aunt Gittel had a bungalow, was just the place; it was only one hour from Lida, with huge pine forests and fresh, clean air. We rented half of a newly-built bungalow a short distance from the village. The bungalow had two apartments. The large porch, onto which the branches of the pine trees persistently encroached, had to be shared with the other family. We had decided on it late, and nothing else was available.

The day we arrived, the workers were still finishing the shutters. The fresh smell of wood and pine permeated the air. The day was sunny and warm. The other family was already there. They turned out to be a nice couple, a schoolteacher from a neighboring town with two small children, a boy of about four and a girl of about one-and-a-half. Each end of the porch had a built-in corner bench and a table. As soon as my father sat down on the bench, the boy ran to him and climbed on his lap. His little sister followed and struggled to get her share of my father's knee. From then on, it became an established routine. Even when the little girl was sitting with her mother, the minute she saw my father, she slipped away and ran to our side of the porch.

We brought along hammocks and fastened them to the trees right beside the house. The moment my father lay down in his, those two little children were on top of him, and, as if from nowhere other children appeared. Like flies attracted to a jar of honey, the hammock became a beehive. They found out something else—his pockets were full of candies. Whenever there were children around, he had candies waiting for them. He let them poke his ears or pull his nose. He caught their little fingers in his mouth, causing them to shriek and laugh. The children had a good time, but my father didn't have his much-needed rest.

We spent our summers in different resorts, such as Pyshki, Novoyelnia, Druskieniki, to name a few. In Pyshki, we had the company of all our Grodno relatives, and those were wonderful summers for all of us. I believe, though, that the best time we had in Pyshki was once on the ride home.

It was probably the only summer that my Aunt Gittel had been persuaded not to return to her beloved Novoyelnia. My mother and Aunt Gittel and my two Grodno aunts had decided to spend the summer together. We stayed in a small hotel and spent the days hiking, relaxing and boating. Uncle Yaakov was abroad, and my father and my Grodno uncles would come for *Shabbos*.

When the summer was over, and it was time to go home, the Grodno cousins and aunts and Uncle Moishe all came to see us and Aunt Gittel off at the train station. When my father travelled himself, he would usually go third class, but for the family he preferred second-class compartments for six, with upholstered seats and curtained windows, clean and quiet. The whole clan helped us with our luggage, and as we opened the sliding door to the compartment, we saw our sixth travelling companion, an elegant Polish lady in a big hat and gloved hands, busy reading her newspaper. Only five of us were travelling, my mother, Aunt Gittel, Sonia, Mendel and I, but on hearing all the commotion of our extended family, the lady looked up with unconcealed rage and anti-Semitism.

"What's all this, are all of you travelling?" she asked with seething anger.

Uncle Moishe, in a mock-serious manner, bowed courteously. "No, most esteemed lady," he said. "A few more people have yet to join us."

It was very funny, and we all burst out laughing. That was the last we heard from our Polish travelling companion, who hid behind her newspaper until we switched trains an hour and a half later.

One summer, we were really fortunate in our choice of a bungalow, this time in Druskieniki. It was a big house with four apartments, each with a separate porch. Druskieniki was only an hour away from Grodno by train, and before the season started, my father had gone there and chosen the best front apartment with the biggest porch. Benches with tables were a standard feature on all summer home porches. Ours could easily seat ten or twelve people.

When we arrived, the other three apartments were already taken. My father was delighted that our next door neighbors were Reb Yerucham Levovitz, the *mashgiach* of the Mirrer Yeshivah, and his family. On the other side, one apartment was taken by two sisters-in-law, the daughter and daughter-in-law of the distinguished Prives family from Warsaw. The fourth apartment was occupied by the prominent Cyrinskis from Vilna; Madame Cyrinski was the daughter of the famous Rabbi Maze from Moscow. My mother enjoyed the company of these ladies to the fullest. At once, she became very close with all the women, and they were truly a select group.

I remember Rebbetzin Levovitz, a short, jolly woman with an easy laugh. It was humorously told that summer how her husband, by failing to be a clever businessman, had become a great *talmid chacham* and famous *mashgiach*. Her parents owned a restaurant, and her father had wanted his young son-in-law to learn a little about the business by helping attend to the customers. The young man did it as he understood it should be done. When he noticed a man rushing in and starting to eat without washing, he would come over and gently remind him, "Reb Yid, you are probably so busy that you forgot to wash before you ate the bread." Once, when he noticed that someone was served a portion of chicken that had been cooked the day before, a widely-accepted practice, he quietly told the man that he should know the chicken was cooked yesterday. His father-in-law promptly sent him back to the *Gemara!*

The summer turned out to be a very sociable one for me as well. My good friend Tania Zhyzhemska, also an only child, came with her mother to Druskieniki year after year, and I was very happy to have her there. Fradka Rabinovitz, the Lida Rav's daughter, Chana Steinberg and a few others also belonged to my circle of close friends. Tania, in particular, was a character. Though she was tall and thin, she joined me in all the slimming programs.

Those days, just a few short years before the war, were happy and content, without a worry or a care.

For my father, the summer vacations were the best time of the year. He particularly liked Druskieniki. It was the only resort place in eastern Poland, and many Lithuanian *rabbanim* and *roshei yeshivah* used to come for mineral baths. Here he was in his element.

This particular summer, though, exceeded every previous expectation. Every afternoon, our porch was converted into a rabbinical council, and so it was jokingly called "the rabbinate." Among the *rabbanim* who gathered there were the old Suvalki Rav, then still called the Semiatitcher Rav, because for many years he was the rabbi in Semiatitch, a town near Warsaw; the Lomza Rav, Rabbi Shatzkes; the Krynka Rav, Rabbi Myshkovski, who was a relative of my father's and a leading rabbinical personality; our own Lida Rav, Rabbi Aaron Rabinovitz; Rabbi Yerucham Levovitz; and many others whose names have escaped my memory.

Another special gathering place for the *rabbanim* was on the long promenade along the Niemen River. The river was on one side, a thick pine forest on the other, and the wide benches along the way provided a cool and relaxing place for Torah *pilpulim*.

The young, modern public preferred the park with its beautiful flowerbeds where a string orchestra played every afternoon. This left the promenade free for the *rabbanim* and the students who had come with them. American *yeshivah* boys with cameras would hide behind the trees and click away at the benches where the *rabbanim* were sitting. As far as I remember, my father was the only "layman" among them. The *yeshivah* boys would later send us the pictures, and my father had a whole collection of them.

I remember my father once telling us how Reb Baruch Ber Leibowitz, the famous *rosh yeshivah* from Kamenitz, caught a *yeshivah* boy in the act of snapping his picture and sternly told him to destroy the film. This moment itself was caught by another boy, though; there was no escaping those cameras! Unfortunately, our photograph albums were confiscated when the Soviets arrested my father. Photographs were important to the Soviets. They were proof of one's associations, they hoped to find incriminating evidence, and they were glad to pick out accomplices to arrest as well.

Another summer, also in Druskieniki, we stayed in the Central Hotel. It turned out that a few doors down the hall, on the same floor, was the suite of Reb Chaim Ozer Grodzenski from Vilna, whom my father knew well. It was a joyous meeting for both. For a whole month, every day from four until six in the afternoon, they were seen walking along the river, engrossed in a *shmuess*. My father was very punctual, and four o'clock on the dot he would knock on Reb Chaim Ozer's door.

It once happened that my father had a visitor and didn't notice the time. A few minutes after four, there was a knock on our door. I was in the room, and I opened the door. Reb Chaim Ozer was known for his extremely sharp, penetrating gaze. I saw eyes like two burning coals and quickly stepped aside as my father went to meet him.

"What happened today? Has our friendship terminated?"

Reb Chaim Ozer asked, but then noticing the guest, he smiled and just said, "Oh."

When we went to Krynitza, a resort at the foot of the Carpathian mountains in Galicia, my father's steady companion was Rabbi Shuster from Sokolka. Their long walks and talks often started right after breakfast. Rabbi Shuster used to give a lecture every day at about five in the afternoon, standing on one of the round tables in the park, drawing a crowd of several hundred people. He spoke several languages and had a broad knowledge of physics, chemistry and philosophy. His topics combined Torah with his general knowledge. The summer before the war, we were again in Krynitza and my father befriended the Jaroslaver Rav, Rabbi Steinberg, a prominent rabbi from Galicia. They also spent long hours in Talmudic discussions.

In my father's youth, it was still common for *talmidei chachamim* to keep their sons at home, teaching them Torah themselves. My grandfather had raised his three sons that way, and all of my father's training in Torah had come from his father, the genius of Grodno. Circumstances had made my father a businessman, but his heart was fully immersed in Torah. He cherished every moment of spiritual elevation from his guests at home and from his revered companions in the summer months.

CHAPTER 14

■

The Doctor's Note

THE MORE I REMINISCED, THE MORE THE PAST BECAME the present for me. It was as if, during my one month in the barn, I experienced my whole previous life anew, including my emotions and reactions. Now it was shattered again into irretrievable fragments by Brodatch's voice. He was standing in the barn door.

"I have just spoken to Ravtzov," he was saying, "and according to him, it is safe for you to come out of hiding. After the first week, there were no more inquiries from the police."

"But where shall I go? I can't go back to Tokushy, as much as I want to see my mother. You forget that I left work without a release. After all this, shall I get arrested and sent to prison?"

"You don't have to worry about your mother," he assured

me. "Etia and Kreina are helping her. Here, I brought a letter from her. I see her often, and she is fine. As far as a place to stay, Ravtzov suggested you come live with his old mother until something more permanent can be arranged. As always, he is ready to help. Here is Ravtzov's address. I paid the woman here until the end of the week.

"Don't worry about the money," he continued, seeing my worried look. "I am keeping an account. You'll pay me back when you get settled. And as always, your money will bring me luck. I have to go now. I'm sure you'll find the way to Ravtzov, but wait until it gets darker."

As always, he was in a rush. I barely had time to scribble a few words to my mother before he was gone.

I sat in my corner, giving thanks to Hashem for the goodness of people who cared. I had not done enough to deserve it. I knew it was in the *zchus* of my father's *chessed* and *tzeddakah* that strangers, particularly a Soviet party member, should show so much concern.

It was completely dark when, exhausted and somewhat unsure of myself, I knocked at Ravtzov's door. His wife, an ample woman in her fifties, opened the door. It was the first time I had seen her. Obviously, she knew I would be coming, because she hurriedly motioned with her hand to the left end of the foyer where her ninety-year-old mother-in-law had a separate room with a tiny kitchenette. From a room to the right of the foyer, I heard several voices talking and laughing.

It was one of the infrequent days when Ravtzov was in Petropavlovsk. He was probably entertaining his party comrades. The old Mrs. Ravtzov was a sight not often seen in Soviet Russia. She was a woman from years gone by, old but healthy and alert. A kerchief tied under her chin covered her head, and her dark dress reached to her ankles. She knew

141

about me, too, because I noticed that beside her bed a couch was prepared for sleeping.

"Come in, come in," she said smiling, obviously happy to have a companion.

A normal bed with clean linen, a room with electricity? Could it be real? I wondered to myself. No rats, no bugs, no cow, no manure! I didn't care if it lasted an eternity or a day. In a land of total brutality and darkness, only miracles can keep one's head above water.

"Put down your bundle over here," the old woman said. "Take off your jacket. Come here and sit down. You are probably hungry. Come, I'll give you something to eat." I did as she told me, still a little dazed by the sudden change in my circumstances. She quickly put some bread, sour cream and boiled eggs on the table, without interrupting her monologue.

"You see, my son is very devoted to me," she was saying. "His wife is also a good woman, but I have to cook for myself. They don't keep kosher! They eat pork, no separate dishes, no *Shabbos*, nothing. That's why my son gave me a separate room with a small kitchen. I eat only dairy. The girl who cleans and works for my daughter-in-law brings me what I request, and she also washes my clothing and the floor. My son has a very high position, and he is not stingy." I knew Ravtzov from Tokushy and the favors he showered on the Jewish exiles. "Eat, eat," she urged me.

I was amazed to discover that Ravtzov had a religious mother, but my thoughts were interrupted by a knock at the door. His company gone, Ravtzov came in to say good night to his mother.

"Oh! You came!" he said, noticing me. "Good. I am leaving tomorrow, early in the morning. While I'm away, you may go out and spend time with my wife also, but when I'm here, stay in this room. The cleaning girl will know you as a visiting relative." In the Soviet heaven, the higher one's position the more one is subject to suspicion.

Ravtzov's wife Gossie, despite her affluence, was a very unhappy person. She hadn't made friends in Petropavlovsk. Her habit of talking too much made her husband wary of letting her have associations. But worst of all, she worried about her two sons in the war. She was like a prisoner kept comfortable and provided for, but lonely and afraid. My short-term stay in their house gave her a chance to unburden herself of her worries and pain. I suspected that when Ravtzov had invited me to stay with his mother, more likely he had had his wife in mind. After a week, he came back to Petropavlovsk.

On his advice and detailed instructions, as well as a loan, I undertook a daring and dangerous plan, which would invoke some tricky playacting. Despair and necessity are the best teachers; they even taught me to put on an act. It was September, 1944.

Before the war, the First Stalinski Hospital had been a government hospital for civilians. It was the biggest in Petropavlovsk, the capital of Northern Kazakhstan, a town between Chelyabinsk and Omsk on the Trans-Asiatic Railroad in Siberia.

During the war, thousands upon thousands of wounded were taken from the battlefields to the safety of the outlying regions of the Soviet Union, including Siberia. All the hospitals were converted to military use. Only in rare emergency cases were civilians also admitted. The brass, of course, had free access to all facilities. There were no private doctors; nothing in Russia was private. The hospitals were badly understaffed, as most of the able-bodied men were drafted into the army.

Dr. Kolaga, the head of the hospital, was about sixty years old and lame, which was why he was assigned to supervise a hospital in a Siberian town. I had had an opportunity to find out a few details about him. First, I discovered that, in a discreet way, he was cooperative. I also discovered that he had recently married a young nurse. It was important that I get to him in order to execute my plan.

The hospital was a big white structure on parklike grounds, about a hundred yards from the street. It was surrounded by a high wire fence, with a booth in front in which a military watchman sat. The gate was opened only to admit transports of wounded. All pedestrians had to enter through the booth. I also learned that family members were permitted to visit, and here is where my acting was to begin.

When I started out, my heart was pounding with uncertainty and fear. I ran the last long block before the hospital, so that when I reached the gate I was breathless; I had rubbed my eyes with onion to make them red and teary. I had also made two long smudges on my cheeks with a dusty finger to appear as if I had been crying, although I had reason enough to cry without acting. Without stopping for a moment, I burst into the sentry's booth.

"Hey, where are you going?" he demanded. "Who are you?"

As if on cue, although this time I wasn't acting, real tears began flowing down my cheeks, and in a breathless, gasping voice, I told him that I had just heard that my only brother had been brought to the hospital badly wounded, with both legs missing. If I couldn't see him immediately, I would probably never see him alive at all. He probably heard stories like this about a hundred times a day.

"Ha, don't worry," he said. "If he made it all the way to Petropavlovsk, he'll live. What is your last name?" The last question was just a formality; he didn't even have a list with him.

I gave him some Russian name, still panting and twisting my fingers. Meanwhile, more people came into the booth. He motioned to the opposite door, and I was on the hospital grounds. I ran the first few yards, then slowed down, wiped my face and began to prepare the second act.

The doctor is not a simple watchman, I thought. Will I succeed? In any case, I had to take the chance; too much depended on it. I clutched my stomach with both hands, bent my right knee, began moaning and, with a face distorted with pain, approached the formidable building. No gleaming walls and floors here. Drab, everything drab, but this was the least of my concerns.

"I must see Dr. Kolaga!" I cried out to the back of a white-clad figure who was arranging something on a hospital cart farther down the hall. As she turned, I leaned against the wall, still moaning as if overcome with pain.

I heard real moaning from several directions. A stretcher with a mummy-like wounded man was wheeled past me. Another patient, with one leg and a crutch, and a hand missing as well, was helped through a door by a woman. Two women crying hysterically, holding on to each other, were leaning against the wall a few steps from me. Misery, everywhere misery. Being in Siberia for four years, I had seen enough misery and death, enough limbless bodies, remnants of what had once been a human being. Too many times I had seen the despair of a wife, mother or children. Crying and moaning had become a way of life for us. And still, the sight in the hospital hallway was utterly depressing.

No distractions now, I told myself. However painful, continue what you have undertaken.

"What's the trouble?" asked a sweet, young voice, striking a dissonant chord amid the woeful noises.

Keeping my eyes half-closed, and with dragged out, choked words, I pronounced, "I have acute appendicitis; it's an emergency. I must see the doctor! I came from Poludieno. The doctor there sent me here."

"Sit down," she said and motioned to one of the benches which ran along both sides of the hall. "The doctor is now at lunch. He'll be back in half an hour."

"I can't wait that long," I said. "I'm dying from pain."

She hesitated for a moment, then she pointed in the direction of a little house with white shutters, visible through the large, bare window in the hall.

"That is where the doctor lives," she said. "You can try to see him there." Then she was instantly off to continue her interrupted work.

I hesitated, but only for a moment. I picked myself up and started in the direction of the white-shuttered house. Five minutes later, a pretty young woman, whom I assumed to be his young wife, opened the door. I repeated my rehearsed statement to her in the same agonized voice.

"Go back to the hospital," she said. "The doctor will see you soon."

I went back to the hospital. Before long, I saw a short, stocky man, dragging a stiff leg, come into the hall. The young nurse was still busy at her cart. The doctor opened a door leading to a room opposite the big window in the hall. I was still sitting doubled over on the bench.

"This girl said she has appendicitis and that she is in great pain," said the nurse, stopping at the open door of the doctor's office.

"Come in, both of you," I heard him say.

A thought flashed through my mind. Both? It meant a witness, and in delicate situations like bribing, witnesses were not desirable. But there was no way out now.

I entered the office. Large and sunny, it contrasted sharply with the drabness of the hall. Between two windows, facing the door, stood a large desk and a high-backed chair. Above the chair hung the inevitable portrait of the bushy-whiskered tyrant Stalin.

Meanwhile, the nurse pulled a curtain at the other end of the room, revealing a high examination table, surprisingly clean and neat, with a stepstool nearby just as in every doctor's office all over the world.

"Give me your *spravka*," he said.

A *spravka* was a kind of recommendation or note from one authority to another which one had to obtain in order to accomplish anything and everything. They were written by whichever authority one was handled by, and they were not easy to obtain. Often, they had to be bought.

Without a *spravka*, or *komandirovka*, one was unable to go from one location to another, no train ticket would be sold, no admission anywhere, to anyplace.

"Of course I have a *spravka*," I claimed, as I started fumbling in my pocket, but all I could produce was a wet handkerchief. My face and bent body still feigned agonizing pain.

"I-I don't know," I said. "I had it in my pocket, but it was such a long way, and I was in pain all the way, and crying, and I probably lost it taking out my handkerchief."

"Lie down," said the doctor. "I'll examine you."

147

I climbed onto the cot. He checked my pulse and pressed my abdomen. I cried out a few times, probably in all the wrong places, and being an experienced doctor and shrewd as well, he saw through the charade. His face, though, remained grave and serious. For a moment, even I believed that something was really wrong.

"Yes, you do have an inflammation. First, I'll have to give you an injection." This was meant for the nurse to hear. He went to a cabinet near his desk and said, "Nadia, please forgive me for keeping you so long. I know how busy you are these days."

The nurse, a sweet, naive girl, gave me a sympathetic look and left the room.

Good, I thought. Now I am on safer ground. I climbed down from the cot, and the doctor, instead of opening the cabinet, sat down at his desk, indicating the chair opposite his.

"What is this all about?" he asked.

He spoke, as I had already noticed before, in short, concise sentences. He knew the general rule that words in Russia are more deadly than a loaded gun. I had also learned something by then, so I did not tell him that I had escaped in the middle of the night from Tokushy, my registered place of residence, that I had been hiding for a full month in a cow barn or that the police and the N.K.V.D. were still after me. I only told him that I presently lived in Tokushy, and that I had an old, sick mother whose health was deteriorating rapidly. Moving to Petropavlovsk was now my only goal, because only in such a big town could I earn enough to support my mother and myself. I also told him that I had left my place of work without permission, which by itself consti-tuted a crime entailing a punishment of up to five years in prison. Of course, being a Soviet citizen, he was familiar with this.

I told him I was from eastern Poland, which had been taken over by the Soviets in September, 1939, and that for the last four years I had been in exile with my mother in Siberia. I told him that I still had some very nice clothing which would be much easier to sell in a big town.

I studied his face and read his thoughts. How much his young wife would appreciate a good foreign-made dress or suit! I thought. Then and there, I resolved to come back soon with a dress for his wife, but afterwards, I was advised by Ravtzov not to return to the hospital. It was more prudent and safer, he believed, never to return to the scene of a crime, such as bribery.

"What shall I write?" he asked, stealing a sideways glance at the heavy paperweight on his desk, which was now wedged up by an envelope I had slid under it, containing a few hundred *chervoncy*. I was still trembling inwardly, not believing I had really heard his question correctly. The events of the past hour and of the preceding few months were reeling in my head like a kaleidoscopic blur. Then I caught sight of his hand holding the pen over a slip of paper, and I came back to reality.

"Please write that I am seriously ill and must be under constant medical care," I said. "A permanent stay in Petropavlovsk is, therefore, vital."

I watched in disbelief as he wrote, signed, affixed the hospital seal on the piece of paper and, with an understanding nod of his head, handed it to me. I thanked him and left his office and the hospital building. I walked down the long path to the gate, through the watchman's booth and into the street.

Now back in the street, I felt suddenly drained and exhausted. There was a bench in front of the hospital fence, and I eased myself onto it, clutching the precious piece of paper in my pocket. Now with the doctor's *spravka*, I'll be able to receive a permit to register in town and bring my mother over, I thought. It wouldn't be so easy, of course. I was still a deserter, a fugitive who had to watch her step and look over her shoulder. But so far, thank Heaven for this.

I was tired. Not hungry, or thirsty, just tired. I leaned back on the bench and closed my eyes. I wanted to sleep. It was a crisp, cool, sunny September day, barely past noon. The air, dense with the fragrance of fallen leaves and drying grass, was fresh and clean. Garbage collection was non-existent. Nothing was thrown out. Everything was saved and used. There wasn't even a piece of paper blown by the wind. It was snatched up from the air by some passerby and pocketed away; if nothing else, it would later be wrapped around a few flakes of coarse tobacco and delightedly inhaled during a moment of relaxation.

I still had my eyes closed when I heard someone sit down on the other end of the bench. My heart jumped. The fear that had accompanied me to the hospital was still in my bones. Fear was an inseparable companion to every human being in Russia. It is the mechanism that makes the regime tick. People were afraid of their own shadows. I had feared, naturally, that I was being watched and followed, that perhaps the doctor would tip somebody off and give me away. Now I was almost sure that he had.

Why hadn't I run from here? Why had I chosen to sit just on this bench? Nonsense, don't be silly, I said to myself. Probably, someone was tired and just wanted to rest. I didn't dare open my eyes. But if someone is really after you, it will not help to play the ostrich sticking his head in the sand, I told myself. Then the person picked himself up and left. I sighed with a surge of contentment. Happiness, after all, is a very relative concept.

CHAPTER 15

---■---

The End of a Chapter

FTER OBTAINING THE DOCTOR'S NOTE STATING THAT I needed constant medical care and, therefore, had to live in Petropavlovsk, I had to find a permanent residence. Without a place to live, there could be no registration in town. I was afraid, however, that registering would bring me to the attention of the K.G.B., but Ravtzov assured me that I could trust him.

A few weeks later, a Soviet refugee lawyer I knew from my previous trips to Petropavlovsk, and whose family I had befriended, explained to me that in order to look for me in Petropavlovsk, the Poludieno K.G.B. would have had to send my records there. That would have shown their double failure—not being able to persuade me to become an informer and not preventing my escape from Tokushy. Thus,

I was fairly safe in Petropavlovsk.

With no apartments available, Liba Shmulovitz and her beautiful daughter Freidele, came to my rescue once more; indeed in times of need, Liba with her outstretched, helping hand always came to our aid. They had moved to Petropavlovsk a year before. After two weeks of Ravtzov's hospitality, Liba offered that I share their room. My name had to be entered in the house record book, with the landlord's triangle seal affixed next to it. Then the doctor's note and the book had to be taken to the *Domuprav*, an office resembling a rent commission, building department and city registry all in one. Surprisingly, it took only a few days to obtain the permit to stay in the city.

At that time, Liba's son Lazar was drafted to work in the coal mines of Karaganda and Liba was allowed to visit him there. Shortly after I came to stay with her, Liba visited Lazar and brought back a blank sheet of paper with the letterhead of the Karaganda coal mines, which Lazar had obtained. Not being very fluent in Russian herself, Liba asked me to write a *"kommandirovka"* for Lazar in the name of the coal mine office, authorizing him to go to Moscow for supplies.

Of course, an official letter of this sort required an official seal, but Liba solved this problem by borrowing the landlord's triangle seal. I dipped the seal in ink and affixed it to the *"kommandirovka."* The words on the seal were illegible, and I scrawled an elaborate, equally illegible signature over it, thereby adding forgery to my growing assortment of trades.

My involvement ended with this, and I never learned the details of what transpired afterwards. I do remember, however, that after the war Liba received a letter from Lazar, postmarked in Poland, in which he stated that he was planning to make his way to Palestine.

As soon as I obtained permission to live in Petropavlovsk, I started to plan moving my mother and our possessions to our new location. It was not easy. I was afraid to go back to Tokushy, and my mother was not able to make the move herself. Until then, all our moves had been arranged by the K.G.B. How was I to organize a move on my own?

By then, the Polish Jewish community in Petropavlovsk was a sizeable one. In addition, there were also many Soviet Jews who were able to escape from the European part of the U.S.S.R., knowing that the Germans, in spite of their initial victories, would never cross the Urals into Siberia. I was constantly asking around among all these people for information on how to hire a truck. It took me a month until I succeeded, and it was, coincidentally, through a niece of our landlord. Her fiance had been wounded in the war and released from the army. He was employed as a truck driver for some cooperative. His job was to deliver supplies to the neighboring villages. I had to wait for his next trip to Tokushy, and when it came I summoned all my courage and climbed into the seat next to the driver. He let me off before we reached the town.

It was the end of October, and the day was cold and windy. I raised my jacket collar, pulled my kerchief low over my forehead and ran to our house. It was one o'clock in the afternoon. I hadn't had a chance to notify my mother, but she had already heard from Brodatch that I was coming and had been waiting for me for a whole month. The driver had told me to be ready in two hours. Luckily, Etia and the boys were home for lunch. With Etia's and Kreina's help, a few big burlap bags filled with produce from our garden were neatly tied and piled up in the first room waiting for the move.

Our clothing and some extra bedding had always been

kept in the trunk and two valises, so now all that was left to do was tie up the bedding from the beds in one of the sheets, put all the pots and dishes inside the bedding so they wouldn't rattle and fold my mother's iron bed. We were ready to move.

The driver arrived half an hour earlier than planned, bringing the truck just in front of our door and across the yard from the windows of the Selsoviet. The driver, Etia, the boys and I were loading our things as if we were running from a fire. It took no longer than ten minutes, and by some miracle, not one of the villagers or the Selsoviet men came to the scene. Amid tears and sighs, we said good-bye to each other.

My mother took her seat in the driver's cabin, and I settled myself on top of the truck among the bags and bundles. When the truck passed the last village house, I realized that a miracle had happened again. In bright daylight, under the nose of the Selsoviet, another chapter of our Siberian experience had come to an end.

Our half room at 8 Octiabrska Street in Petropavlovsk wasn't too comfortable, but neither was Liba's half. The room was small, and we had more possessions than Liba, so it was a real sacrifice on her part to take us in. Of course, we shared the rent and, the most important thing in Siberia, the firewood. When we arrived in the late afternoon, it was snowing, and though the first sparrow doesn't bring the spring, the October snow in Siberia does mean the start of winter.

Regardless of the clutter and sardine-like squeeze, the small room had important advantages—a private entrance from the vestibule and electricity! What a great luxury!

Unfortunately, it didn't have the regular Russian oven, which would have kept the room warm many hours after it stopped burning. Instead, there was only a small, two-burner kitchen stove, which could use coal or wood and had to be constantly fed. A special, unexpected luxury was a wall outlet and a radio speaker hung high on the wall under the ceiling.

Although the outlet was for the radio speaker, we soon discovered that we could use the outlet for another purpose, too. Through selling clothing, I made contacts with a few wives of higher officials, and one of them gave me an old, little electric stove. What a find! In the winter, we kept the fuel-burning stove going most of the day, in any case, but in the summer, we could cook without using up fuel! We could save fuel for the winter and keep the apartment cool, as well. The wire was short and broken, but Liba knew an electrician who was able to fix it.

Before we had time to look around, the winter set in with all its force. The old struggle to keep the place warm, or rather, above freezing, and to satisfy our constant hunger started all over again. In fact, the struggle was a continuous one, but when I had been forced to work by the K.G.B. or in the *artel*, we had at least had our daily rations of bread. In Petropavlovsk, it was easy enough to find a job, but a job invariably meant having to work on *Shabbos*. So I had to look for other sources of income.

The few bags of potatoes and other vegetables we had brought from Tokushy were quickly gone. Our room was too small to accommodate all our possessions, so our landlady had graciously offered the space behind the oven in her big kitchen for our vegetable sacks. She lived in the kitchen with her husband and a refugee woman with a small child. Past the kitchen was another room where two families minus the husbands lived. They always asked if they could borrow a few potatoes or a carrot, and I couldn't refuse. As a result, the stock quickly ran out.

After selling a few pieces of clothing to raise money to repay my debts, and going to the *baracholka*, the peddlers' market place, to buy some edibles, I noticed that besides the peasant women selling their garden produce, others, mostly women, were selling and buying all kinds of items.

In all of Petropavlovsk there were three or four stores, usually closed. There was a newspaper stand in the center of town, but no matter how early one came, the curled up invalid behind the stand had one answer, "All sold." There was also an *apteka*, a drug store, where prescriptions were filled, always the "next day" or "the day after next." The only place that thrived was the beauty parlor, where two hairdressers and a manicurist were busy around the clock. The wives of the brass wanted to be pretty. Coming from the lower classes, they considered red nails and curly mops the ultimate in status and elegance.

There was also a fairly big commissary where people could bring whatever used items they wanted to sell, from clothing to housewares. Of course, it was also government-owned, but the prices were higher than for government items, which were never available anyway. The maximum length of time an item was kept was three months. Thus, the *baracholka* (from *barachlo*—junk) was the only place where the turnover was from hand to hand. Officially, only used items or clothing were permitted, but under a coat or shawl, a piece of stolen material, sewing thread, leather for soles and other such basic necessities quickly changed hands before a policeman could spot the transaction.

In Petropavlovsk, there were two *baracholkas*, and Liba

frequented both, buying in one and selling in the other. If such behavior was caught, it was severely punished—*spekulantka*, capitalist speculator! Besides politics, it was the most offensive crime in Soviet Russia, carrying the penalty of ten years in a labor camp. Stalin allowed himself the privilege of chopping off the heads of his own comrades and thousands of innocents, but to "speculate" in order to feed hungry children while the father was away in the army defending the homeland, possibly wounded or killed, was considered a terrible crime.

Being unable to get a job without working on *Shabbos*, I joined the delinquent crowd. I became a *spekulantka*, though of a somewhat different variety. Rather than showing my face too often in the *baracholka*, where policemen and informers were constantly circulating, I chose knocking on doors. For a start, I took a few things my mother and I could do without and went out to try my luck. Many people were suspicious and didn't even want to open the door. The more brave, seeing that I offered "western" goods, grabbed them eagerly. Some bought for money, others offered something in exchange. In the *kolkhoz*, all the barters had been for food, but here in town, money was very welcome. The best trade-in I remember was a pair of new, high rubber boots, which Aunt Etie had sent during the first year, in exchange for a portable, hand-operated sewing machine. It was very old and rusty, like its owner, but it began a new chapter in my career.

Happy and excited, I brought it home. After lumber and grain loading and railroad-building, it seemed easy to carry a sewing machine all that way. Before the deal was made, the old woman showed me how to operate it. It screeched and clacked, but it did sew. At home, after a thorough inspection and advice from our landlady, it was decided that it needed a good oiling to reduce the noise. There was no machine oil, and the cooking oil, dark, thick, and unrefined, would clog the parts and do more harm than good.

"Kerosene will do," was the landlady's verdict. "Wait until my niece comes. She'll ask her fiance. He'll get it."

What was easy in other parts of the world had to be sweated out with pain and patience in Russia.

To practice I took an old sheet, cut out the middle part where it was worn thin as cheesecloth, dyed the sides which were still sturdy and produced two skirts. Style and size notwithstanding, I took one to the *baracholka*. To have brought both would have meant mass production—ergo, *spekulantka*! With only one, I didn't have to hide it, as it surely didn't look new, but it went quickly enough. From then on, I was mostly in the skirt business. I made dozens of them. They were easy to sew (one size fits all) and easy to sell. I used any material I could lay my hands on, except for silk and velvet, even khaki colored army tent canvas, stolen by some soldier and sold on the market by his wife or mother. My old machine groaned but obeyed.

Once, I got a real find. One of the women I had dealt with a few times before secretly informed me that she had gotten hold of a rare and excellent piece of material, cream colored and very strong.

"There's only one thing," she said. "It doesn't take dye."

"Show it to me," I said.

She led me to her bedroom and pulled a huge, oddly-shaped piece of material from under her bedcovers. It was smooth and silky to the touch, and I noticed that it was cut from some bigger piece, probably with a knife or a razor blade. It hit me that it must have been part of a parachute, although I had never seen one. I told her what I suspected.

159

She paled and almost went into shock. There is a dual quality in the character of Russian people, a shrewdness and foxy cleverness, and an almost childish naivete. The sound of the word parachute brought out an almost hysterical fear in her.

"I didn't know," she cried out. "I never would have bought it, even though it was cheap. I would never have bought it."

She had bought it for next to nothing, probably from a soldier who had been able to hide it in his backpack, and who was afraid of being caught and wanted to get rid of it quickly. I bought it, also for very little, but it was so big that we both had to struggle to roll it up tightly to make a bundle as small as possible.

"You shouldn't use it right away," my mother cautioned me wisely, and so it rested for a while under our bedding.

The tent canvas and the piece of parachute silk weren't the only things which I had the opportunity to buy through a Russian soldier returning from Europe. One morning at the market, I saw a soldier who looked like he had something to sell. Approaching him, he told me he had a very special item, something almost unseen in Siberia, a bar of facial soap. I wasn't surprised, because in many cases soldiers returning from Europe would bring looted or stolen goods of greater value than a bar of soap.

I asked him to show it to me. He took it out of his coat pocket, and as I took it in my hand, a shudder went through my body. It was stamped with a big, heavy "J." We had heard about such bars of soap. We knew how the Germans made them. The shocking fact was that they cooked Jewish bodies for the fat to make the soap.

Looking at it with eyes clouded with tears and horror, I could see in it pieces of my murdered aunts and uncles and cousins. It was the first time I had seen any of this soap.

During the last year in Siberia, we used to buy these bars of soap at every opportunity, asking every soldier in the market if he had one. On the train back to Poland, our transport collected twenty-seven such bars, which were taken by someone travelling to Lodz to bury in the Jewish cemetery there.

CHAPTER 16

■

Victory and New Questions

TOWARDS THE END OF 1944, WITHOUT ANY CONTACTS and without applying for them in any way, some Jewish families who in one way or another had been connected with rabbinic circles before the war, began receiving packages from the United States. The sender was Vaad Hatzalah in New York. The packages were addressed to the places where we had originally been sent at the beginning of May, 1940. My mother and I were among the recipients. The Soviets, triumphant with their victories and their having been joined by the Allies in fighting the Germans, allowed the parcels to reach their addressees.

No notices were sent. When news about mysterious packages began to circulate, we thought it was some plot or trick of the K.G.B. Then a few people without "criminal" records like mine went to the post office, and there they were—a shelf full of packages! Someone noticed my name on a package, I decided to take the risk and claim it. Using my permit to live in Petropavlovsk as my identification, I retrieved the package without mishap.

All the parcels were identical, though each shipment, sent about once a month, had different contents. Mine was addressed in clear, Russian print to the *kolkhoz* Sergeyevka, where we had spent our first year. The same address was on all subsequent parcels. On orders from above, if the addressee was no longer in the place to which it was sent, the parcel went to the district center, in our case Poludieno. After a certain time, if nobody claimed it, it was sent to the county seat, in our case Petropavlovsk. In the winter months, when the snow and blizzards delayed the transfers from place to place, two or three parcels would arrive at one time.

All summer long, the American parcels arrived more or less regularly, and they were a tremendous help. The Vaad Hatzalah in New York really knew what was needed. A typical parcel of clothing contained a grayish-navy or khaki colored pullover (man's only, army surplus), a plaid hooded jacket and an army blanket. Sometimes warm underwear was also included. A food parcel might contain a kilo of cocoa, a bottle of saccharin (one thousand grains), a kilo of candies (inferior quality), sugar and rice. Then there were parcels containing bars of laundry soap and parcels containing half kilo packages of loose tea. The tea was made to order for the Kazakhs, the native Asian Muslims we had met during our stay in the railroad camp. In Petropavlovsk, they were my only tea customers. They were willing to travel for tens of kilometers to town, usually with all of their wives and children, just to procure some tea.

I usually took only one item a day to the *baracholka*, and thus one morning I found myself there with a single package of tea half hidden under my shawl. The Kazakhs have a special instinct for finding their "gold," and in no time, many of them were pulling at my hand. Greedy fingers tore open the package, took a few grains and started to chew. Everyone was an expert, and everyone had to give his opinion. The commotion didn't escape the attention of a policeman, however. When he appeared, carrying a rifle, of course, all the Kazakhs vanished into thin air, and I found myself being led away with a half-empty package of tea in my hand. My mother heard about it even before I reached the police station. Someone had seen me and had run to tell her what had happened.

The police station looked like a Siberian railroad waiting room, with the distinction that the windows had bars. Dozens of people, mostly women, were sitting on the floor, holding onto baskets and bundles, wringing their hands, eyes filled with panic. They were waiting to be interrogated. There were two policemen in the room. One was at the door to the interrogator's room, the other watching the entrance door. My policeman, after delivering me, left to hunt for another *spekulantka*.

I sat down on the floor next to a woman who seemed to be more agitated and frightened than the rest. Like all of us, she was wearing a shawl, and under it, in a basket, she had a little notions store—a few spools of thread, a few small plastic combs, some pins and two or three more items of a similar nature. She recognized that I was Jewish and, in a hushed voice choked with tears, kept repeating in Yiddish, "*Oy vey!* At home I have more stuff! If they search there, I'll go to prison! What will happen to my children? My husband is in the army.

I am a refugee here, and I have nobody! *Oy vey, Oy vey!*"

I was miserable myself, but her pain eclipsed mine. I wanted to comfort her, but how? She was a Soviet citizen, and she knew what to expect for such a crime.

The entrance door opened frequently with more and more arrestees filling the room. It became so crowded that there was barely enough place to stand. I noticed that the people who were let in to the interrogator's room didn't come out.

"There is another door from there leading outside," a woman sitting in front of me informed me. "For others, the door leads straight to the prison."

"Silence!" boomed the policeman, hearing the hushed voices coming from our corner.

I never found out what happened to the poor woman who was so desperate; her turn came before mine.

It was completely dark outside, and the gleam from the electric bulb gave a reddish reflection to the straw-haired man across the table, whose water-colored eyes looked at me with hatred and suspicion.

"Why do you have American tea? Do you have any family or friends there?"

"No, I have nobody in America."

"Who sent you the tea? Did you ask for it?"

"No, I have never written to America. The parcel I received was sent by some organization."

"What else was in the parcel?"

"Tea, soap and sugar."

"Was it sent for your own use or for speculation?"

"What I didn't use myself, I wanted to trade for flour."

"Why don't you work?"

"I have a sick mother, and I have to take care of her."

"How many more packages of tea do you have in your house?"

"Only one more," I said, although I had about twelve.

At this point, I decided to take a chance. I knew that if I showed fright or nervousness, it would only make him more suspicious. Instead of continuing to answer his questions, I began insisting that he send policemen to search my room. It worked. Usually, the *spekulants* feared a search more than anything else, and there I was insisting he should order one!

"This time I'll let you go," he said. "But if you get caught again selling anything in the *baracholka*, you'll be arrested right away!" From nine o'clock in the morning until ten o'clock at night, the only thing that mattered in Russia was my half-empty package of tea!

The next day, I did go to the *baracholka*, but empty-handed. I told the first Kazakh I met that I had *tchai* (tea) and motioned toward the exit. He understood and followed me. When we came to the house where I lived, I told him to wait in the yard. I brought out a package but didn't let him touch it. After the customary bargaining, he agreed to bring a *pud* (sixteen kilos) of flour for each package. In this way, we had bread the whole winter, and the Kazakhs had their "tea party." I always wondered how the Kazakhs were able to steal so much grain and not get caught.

The next most valued products in the packages were the cocoa and saccharin. None of my customers for these commodities, though, was ready to buy a whole bottle of saccharin or a whole pound of cocoa, so I had to divide them into smaller quantities. Saccharin was bought by the grain. Little packets made from newspaper containing five or ten grains were the norm. These were usually bought by average Soviet refugees. Cocoa, also in little packets, two or four teaspoons in each, went to the wives of the officials. They found out about my cocoa from each other and would come to our house. Oh, their terrible disappointment if they were told that all of it was gone, and that they would have to wait until the next parcel arrived! But we were never sure what the next parcel would contain. Five years had passed, and the roles had changed. In Sergeyevka I used to wade in slush and mud, knocking on doors for a few onions or potatoes. Here in Petropavlovsk, the manicured ladies knocked on my door for a few teaspoons of cocoa. It was all the same pettiness, in spite of the differences. The officials had excellent rations, and they were bursting from overeating. Only cocoa was missing.

The winter of 1944-1945 came to an end. The triumphant march of the Soviet army had started much earlier, and the bulletins which came from our speaker announced the liberation of one town after another. In time, towns in Poland began to be mentioned, towns which I knew, where I had friends and family. And then one day, loud and clear, came the name of the town of Lida.

It was a bright and sunny day. I looked at the wall, then back at the speaker, thinking that maybe something more would be revealed. They had named my town, my hometown, where I was born and had grown up. How could they continue on without any further details? My heart jumped and sank alternately. From the few refugees way back in 1941, and later from the wounded soldiers sent home, we knew that the path of the Nazi army was strewn with destruction and death, but a spark of hope still flickered. In my mind's eye, I saw my young cousins surrounding me on my return, welcoming me as a heroine, the survivor of a Siberian exile. How naive, silly and egotistic! How could I have compared the hell of a Nazi death camp with Siberia? Siberia was also hell, yet

167

there was no comparison. But we didn't know that yet.

After hearing that Lida was in Soviet hands again, I immediately sent a letter to Uncle Shmuel and Aunt Gittel.

About two months passed before a letter came back. It was postmarked in Lida. On the return address was the name Leibush Ferdman. I knew Leibush Ferdman. He was a professional electrician. For as long as I could remember, he had done all the electrical work in our factory and in our house. His family had perished, but he had survived in a partisan group. With trembling hands, I opened the letter and read:

"As Lida was razed to the ground," he wrote, "and no Jews remained, with the exception of those few who hid in the forests with the partisans, the hundreds of letters which had started to arrive from Russia were all delivered to the temporary city hall. The survivors in Lida were allowed to browse in case there would be a letter for them. I found your letter, but with sorrow I must tell you that no one from your family survived. Your Uncle Shmuel and his family were sent to the death camp of Yanov, not far from the town of Slonim. Your Aunt Gittel was in the Lida ghetto until May 8, 1942, when five thousand five hundred Jews were shot after digging huge, trench-like graves for themselves on the outskirts of the town called Piaski." I couldn't continue reading. The pain was too overwhelming.

My letters to Grodno, Vilna and Bialystok remained unanswered. There was nobody left to read them. It is impossible to relate the numbing pain, the helplessness, the despair we felt in those months.

Changes took place in the world at large, too. We heard, coming from our speaker, the news about President Roosevelt's death. We heard Vice President Truman's oath when he became president. "In G-d we trust," he had said.

It was hard to believe that Soviet radio had allowed the name of G-d to be broadcast. Under Stalin's rule, it was unthinkable. The broadcasts also reported the Allies' bombardment of Berlin; the Soviets' march through Poland to Hungary, Czechoslovakia and the rest of Eastern Europe; and the final surrender of Germany on May 8, 1945, three years to the day after their slaughter of the Jews of Lida.

World War II had come to an end. The Soviets were jubilant. It was said that twenty million Soviet people were killed in the war. For the Soviets, one thousand or one million are just numbers with a few zeros more or less. People were not important. The only thing that was important to them was the spread of Communism over a third of Europe and their growing influence in many other parts of the world.

Poland was arguably one of the most important countries in our long *galus*, where Jewish life bloomed for centuries. Great Torah luminaries lived in Poland and influenced generations of *talmidei chachamim*. All aspects of Jewish genius found their expression in Poland, penetrating the wall of anti-Semitism and hatred. But although Poland was my birthplace, I have very little sentiment for that country and its people. Their treatment of Jews, both during the war and after, was so inhuman that any feelings I might have had for them were completely destroyed. I had absolutely no desire to return to Poland.

In the meantime, the events in the outside world bypassed us. Our status was still that of exiles. It even seemed that our situation took a turn for the worse. Our part of eastern Poland was now incorporated into Soviet Russia as a permanent province and we had become unwilling Soviet citizens. Would they keep the "easterners" in Siberia forever?

Or would they send us back to our burned-down towns to live among the Poles, whose anti-Semitism, enhanced and strengthened by the Germans, would make life a danger and a hell? The war was over, but its residue lingered on like the unmelted snow of early spring. The future looked bleak.

CHAPTER 17

■

A Taste of Soviet Paradise

THE SUMMER OF 1945, SHORT LIKE ALL OTHER SIBERIAN summers, brought a change in my mother's and my living conditions. The room which we had been sharing with Liba and Freidele was too small for four people. Because of our need and the impending winter, Liba had graciously extended her hospitality and squeezed us into their room. But now it was time to move on.

In my wanderings around Petropavlovsk, I had come upon an elderly couple named Kagan who lived at 154 Stalinska Street in a big, well-kept house. It had a big yard with a detached barn, a true Siberian status symbol, and a porch, a foyer and three other rooms. They didn't need any of the items I offered for sale, but when I asked if they had a room for rent, they both answered, simultaneously, "Yes, but on

171

one condition. Two hundred *chervoncy* a month, paid in advance and four cubic meters of firewood brought before you move in."

Here was the crux of the matter, I thought. No wonder they had said it in unison, they had probably repeated it many times. "Four cubic meters of firewood!" I repeated, astounded. If they had asked me to bring down the sky, my reaction would have been the same.

"I'll try to get the wood," I said. "If I succeed, I'll come back." I liked the room, the house was clean and very bright, but the terms were out of reach.

I'm sure Hashem keeps a certain number of miracles for everyone in times of dire need. Once again, the *shaliach* was Ravtzov. I myself didn't have the courage to approach him with such a request, but Brodatch, who often visited us when he was in Petropavlovsk, asked him outright for help with the firewood.

"No problem," Ravtzov said. "Let them rent the room. The wood will be delivered."

I ran to the Kagans with two hundred *chervoncy* in my pocket. I made a deal with them that we would move in, and if during the first two weeks the wood would not be delivered, we would move out. I knew that Ravtzov's word was like a promissory note. Friends who lived nearby, a very fine family called Svietytzki, also exiles, were very helpful in finding a man with a wagon and helping to move our belongings. In a few days, to the bewildered astonishment of Mr. Kagan, a huge wagon with two cubic meters of excellent birch firewood drove into the yard, depositing it on the ground.

"I have an order to deliver two more meters tomorrow," the driver said and drove off. Wood was Ravtzov's official business, although extracurricular deliveries like these, which were probably made regularly to all the government establishments and their bosses in Petropavlovsk, were not quite part of the regular job description.

From that day on, the Kagans showed a special respect for my mother and me. We were given the first room, the bigger one. It was big enough to allow a makeshift partition to be made from sheets, so we had privacy, and the Kagans had undisturbed passage to their room.

The Kagans were also exiles but for another reason, from another time and by a different tyrant. Mr. Kagan had been a young revolutionary when the first attempt to overthrow the Czar's regime in 1905 had been aborted, and the participants were sent to Siberia in chains. The system had since changed, but the methods were the same. After serving his time, he decided to remain in Siberia. His young fiancee joined him, and they settled in Petropavlovsk. After the Communist revolution, Kagan, with his "clean" Communist record, got a job as a supervisor of a cooperative. His ideals fulfilled, he was happy.

If their name hadn't been Kagan, I wouldn't have had any clue to their being Jews, as there was no trace of Jewishness in their lifestyle. I was shocked when I first entered their room to see, prominently displayed, a portrait of Stalin flanked on both sides by framed photographs of Kagan's parents. His father was a Jew with a big *yarmulka* and a long beard, and his mother wore an old-style wig called a *peruk,* which covered her forehead almost to the eyes. A *frum*, old-world couple.

"My father was a *shochet* and a Talmudist," Mr. Kagan said with sarcasm, seeing my puzzled look.

Though I knew I had to be careful with Soviet people, I couldn't contain myself from saying, "You must be proud of your parents."

173

"Proud?" he cried out. "I am proud to be a party member. I am proud of serving a prison term for the cause of Communism. I am proud of my *rodina*, my homeland, which was the first of all countries to accomplish and realize the ideals of Marx and Lenin. I am proud of the fact that I, the son of a poor *shochet* in a small Ukrainian town, became a director of a big cooperative. I am proud that my daughter is finishing medical school and will become a doctor this coming spring. Be proud of ignorant, backward people with their medieval ways? Ha!"

"So why do you keep their pictures on the wall?" I could not help asking.

"To remind me of how I'd look if I had followed in their path," was his terse reply.

"I'm glad to hear that you are happy," I said. "It is so refreshing to see happy people." I remembered his happiness when the firewood had been delivered; he and his wife had been very anxious for firewood, which was no longer attainable for him since he retired.

Mr. Kagan's words about the Soviets' great achievement in realizing the ideals of Marx and Lenin and their worship of Stalin were the product of typical Soviet propaganda. I had heard those words so many times that they were coming out of my ears. What shocked me so forcibly was Mr. Kagan's denigration of his parents.

The door to their room was open and my mother had heard the conversation. When they were out of earshot, I couldn't contain my dismay any longer.

"Mama, how can a Jew's hatred of his own religion and heritage and his own parents lower him to such a degree?"

My mother looked into my pain-filled eyes with calm, patient understanding.

"Yes, it is very painful," my mother said. "It is all the result of our long *galus*. After two thousand years of being dispersed throughout the world, many of our people—too many, I'm afraid—have come to believe that by adopting the ways and lifestyles of the lands in which they live they will endear themselves to the gentiles and be spared our troubles. It hasn't helped them, though. Millions of Jews have brought destruction upon themselves in the name of progress, culture, civilization, enlightenment and materialism. Jews have contributed immensely to all of these ideals, but they have been rewarded with pogroms, blood libels and expulsions. And what is happening now, in our time . . ."

My mother's voice started to quiver and her eyes glazed over with tears. She remained silent for a few moments. A memory flashed through my mind of my mother in our house in Lida engrossed in a discussion about the rise of anti-Semitism in Poland. But my mother wasn't going to let me daydream. She collected herself and continued.

"Jews were given a priceless gift," she said quietly. "But many have exchanged the diamond for a worthless bauble."

"Yes, Mama. How true it is. Have you heard how Mr. Kagan prides himself on being a Communist Party member while he couldn't even get a few pieces of wood to warm his house?" Could a person who had lived in Communist Russia through its worst years be so blind to its complete breakdown of all moral and ethical values? What kind of paradise had the realization of the Communist ideals brought? Destruction, bloodshed, hunger and misery! These questions whirled in my mind, when I heard my mother's words again.

"Hashem gave us another treasure," she was saying, "but we have evidently misused it—*bechirah*, free will. We have to pray and beg Hashem to enable us to make the right choices and select the right priorities."

My mother had touched on the essential point again, as she always did, and I was left with more to think about than I had expected. Rather than wonder about people like the Kagans, she reminded me again that there was still a great deal of work for us to do on ourselves.

A few weeks later, an incident with a chicken proved another example of the paradise in which the Kagans lived.

As in all households in Petropavlovsk, the yard of the Kagans wasn't for idle decoration. In fact, in my six years in Siberia, I didn't see a single flower anywhere. The Kagan's yard was planted with vegetables, with a space for the chicken to peck. They also kept a cow in the barn. These were their main sustenance. The Kagan's life was more similar to that of peasants in a *kolkhoz* than to anything else. One evening, I overheard them discussing a gray chicken.

"You know," said the wife. "The gray chicken didn't lay any eggs the whole summer long. She eats well and seems to be healthy. I don't know the reason."

"She is too old," her husband said. "That's why."

It was almost five and a half years since my mother and I had tasted any kind of meat. In Petropavlovsk, there was an old *shochet*, a relic from pre-World War I days. I don't know if he ever had a chance to use his *chalef*. Kosher *shechitah* was illegal altogether. Besides, I never saw a live chicken being sold on the market. Now, this unexpected combination of a live chicken being available coupled with the presence of the old *shochet* presented a singular opportunity.

"*Rosh Hashanah* is approaching. Maybe you should ask Mrs. Kagan if she wants to sell the chicken to us," suggested my mother when I told her about the conversation. "We'll keep her until *Yom Kippur*, and for the first time in six years, we'll be able to *shlog kaparos*."

Our landlady was always willing to sell milk and eggs; after all, the cow was their main source of sustenance, why shouldn't it provide a little income, too? But a chicken?

I asked her.

"I'll think it over," she answered.

The proverbial question, a little altered, was heard now in their daily, hushed conversations.

"To sell, or not to sell?"

"Maybe she'll start laying eggs again. Maybe it's just a temporary problem."

A difficult decision to make! *Rosh Hashanah* and *Yom Kippur* passed without a deal. Our meals on *Sukkos* were also *milchig*. Then late in October, Mrs. Kagan noticed that the chicken was becoming thinner and losing her appetite. Her husband was right. The chicken was too old.

"If you want the chicken, I'll sell it to you," she said in a resigned tone.

"Mama, through all the holidays since we left Lida we have never had any meat. Should we buy the chicken now?" I asked. It seemed an extraordinary luxury in our reduced surroundings.

"Even after the *churban* of the Beis Hamikdash, *Chazal* advised us to go on with normal life!" my mother exclaimed. "Isn't *kavod Shabbos* enough reason to buy a chicken?"

I bought it and took it to the *shochet*. He slaughtered it secretly in a little shed behind his house. I *kashered* it in the barn.

We had some *fleishige* dishes that Aunt Etie had brought to the station in Lida at the time we were exiled. They were packed away in a bundle, as we hadn't had any use for them all those years. We still had our little electric stove, and we did all our cooking in our room. We used their big, clay, kitchen oven only to bake bread. These ovens, like those in the Sergeyevka *kolkhoz*, were automatically *kashered* thoroughly every time they were started up for baking.

There was no need for a refrigerator in Siberia, especially from the beginning of October until the middle of May. All houses in the towns and *kolkhozy* had outside storage sheds where food was kept. I cut the chicken into an endless number of pieces, wrapped them accordion-like in a towel and overnight they were rock hard. For a long time, we had meat for *Shabbos*. Two legs and the neck, an onion and a few potatoes made an excellent *cholent*.

CHAPTER 18

---■---

A Special Doctor

THE SEVEN MONTHS MY MOTHER AND I LIVED IN THE Kagan house could have been the best, but they turned out to be the most traumatic.

To be sure, we lived in an airy, bright room, heated adequately by a large, floor-to-ceiling, tile-covered oven. Our combined sources of livelihood—Vaad Hatzalah parcels, my sewing and knitting, trading, door-to-door buying and selling—kept us fed and warm. We had a good relationship with our landlords, never mentioning politics and rarely religion. They were helpful when needed, and I reciprocated by knitting for Mrs. Kagan.

We occasionally had visitors whenever time allowed, usually on *Shabbos*. We met the family of Rabbi Levi Belitzki, with whom we became very close. We also visited with Mrs.

Baikalski, who had moved with her family to Petropavlovsk, Dora Kaplinska, the Hurvitzes and a few others. Liba and Freidele used to come over. We shared our worries and our hopes, and the togetherness made life more bearable.

My mother never showed emotion when confronted with bad news, hardship or pain. She was always calm and level-headed, always in full control of the situation at every moment. It seemed that all the tragedies and miseries we had gone through since the beginning of the war were suppressed by her unusually strong will power, and they didn't show in any outward signs. Her strong belief in *hashgachah pratis* was the main factor.

Physically, she had never been strong. She had survived the chokingly crowded living conditions, the numbing cold of the railroad labor camp and the days when our only food was a thin, grayish liquid made from a few tablespoons of flour cooked in rationed water. But now that our situation had become more bearable, the dam gave way.

The news of the annihilation of our entire family was the last straw. One day in November, my mother woke up with high fever and pain in her abdomen. Mrs. Kagan had a rubber hot-water bottle, which I applied, but the pain persisted. I had a few packets of aspirin. This lowered the temperature, but only temporarily. How could I get a doctor? There were no private doctors. All the hospitals in town were still filled with war casualties. For the civilian population there was only a polyclinic, a place where patients were checked, given a prescription and sent home.

One possibility we eliminated was Dr. Kupitzki, a Jewish man in his fifties, a native resident of Petropavlovsk. His father had been a rich merchant, but not rich enough to live outside the Pale of Settlement. He had been caught by the

Czar's gendarmes in St. Petersburg and exiled to Siberia without the right to return. During the reign of Czar Alexander III and Czar Nicholas II, this law applied only to Jews. Dr. Kupitzki, for some transgression, had lost his license to practice medicine. The Kagans told me that he was an excellent doctor but he would never take the risk of seeing a patient. There was also a doctor who was a Polish exile, but he didn't have a Soviet license to practice medicine.

"You can't take your mother to the polyclinic!" Mrs. Kagan advised. "The waiting line is three or four blocks long. People come in the middle of the night to wait for it to open. With such a high fever and pain and in such cold weather, it's too dangerous. Go tomorrow, early in the morning, and when you're admitted, ask for a doctor to be sent home. They used to do this."

I left the house when it was still dark. The Kagans lived far from the center of town, and when I arrived at the polyclinic, it was just as my landlady had said. I had to go three blocks back to take my place at the end of the line.

The biting wind was the worst. The line behind me grew, and the wall of people in front of me gave at least a little protection from the wind. We were stamping our feet, and a thin cloud of steam wavered above our heads from the sighs of the sick and restless.

When my turn finally came, I tearfully begged the girl behind the desk to send a doctor to see my mother. She was impatient with me and showed no desire even to listen to what I had to say.

"We have many sick people. If your mother can't come here, let her stay in bed until she gets better," was the young woman's highly professional advice.

"*V'chom dela?*" I heard a voice ask. "What is it all about?"

I turned and saw a dark-haired, bespectacled, portly woman approaching. I repeated my plea.

"I am Dr. Siegal," she said. "Give me your address. Between four and five this afternoon, I'll come myself."

When I returned home, I found Mrs. Kagan near my mother's bed. With a worried look, she put her finger to her mouth, indicating that I shouldn't talk. I took a look at my mother, and my heart sank. Her face was dark yellow. In a while, she opened her eyes, and they were the same color. She was delirious and didn't recognize me.

One hour, two hours—how long an hour can stretch when you want it to rush by! Every few minutes, I ran to the window, hoping that by some miracle the doctor would come early.

The wind stopped, and a dense, lethargic snow fell incessantly. Even the snow had a yellow tint. Everything I looked at seemed to be yellow.

"In two more hours the snow will be half a meter high," I said to Mrs. Kagan. "How will Dr. Siegal be able to walk such a long way?"

"What? Dr. Siegal herself will come? You must be mistaken. She's the head of the polyclinic. She never makes visits herself. She sends one of the other doctors."

"I spoke to her, and she said she would come herself," I insisted.

"Impossible." Mr. Kagan, who had heard the conversation, upheld his wife's view.

When Mr. Kagan opened the door at five in the afternoon and saw Dr. Siegal, his face showed the same astonishment it had shown when the wagon with wood had arrived. The sled driver who brought the doctor asked permission to wait in the kitchen until the doctor was ready to leave.

Dr. Siegal examined my mother thoroughly, and her

diagnosis was a severe inflammation of the liver. She gave my mother an injection, and the next morning she sent a nurse with medicines. The nurse also drew some blood for an analysis.

Mr. Kagan's eyes almost popped out of their sockets when he saw the nurse handing me the medicine. It would have taken three days to fill the prescription at the *apteka*.

"*Chto ty? Podkupila tvoyevo B-ga?*" he asked incredulously. "What's with you? Did you bribe your G-d?"

He was beside himself—I couldn't tell if it was wonder or anger. My mother and I were exiles, which meant enemies of the Soviet people. How could undesirable elements have such privileges?

"Yes," I said, not wanting to miss an opportunity to make a point. "We did bribe Hashem. With prayer, observing *Shabbos*, not eating *treife* and trying to observe all the other commandments in the most unfavorable conditions."

"Nonsense!" he said and went outside to shovel the snow.

Hashem had sent us an angel in the person of Dr. Siegal. I gave my mother the medicine every four hours, day and night, in a tablespoon of warm milk, as the doctor ordered. The pain subsided a little and the temperature fell, but the yellow color didn't pale. In a few days, Dr. Siegal's sled again stopped in front of the house. She had the results of the blood test and had brought additional medicine. She also ordered a very light diet. Luckily, I had farina which I got in exchange for cocoa, and I cooked it in water mixed with a little milk until it was almost transparent.

For a whole month, Dr. Siegal came twice a week to check on my mother's condition. She had a sled and driver at her disposal, and in the evening after the polyclinic closed, she took the trouble to come to us. With Hashem's help, and Dr.

Siegal's devotion and exclusive care, my mother's condition began to improve. After six weeks in bed, she felt strong enough to walk around, though she still couldn't go outside. In the meantime, Dr. Siegal became our close friend, and she would drop in whenever she had time, both professionally and socially.

She told us her life story. She was about fifty years old, had never married and had come to Siberia a few years before as a war refugee from Kiev. Before the war, she had been a professor of medicine in the University of Kiev. In Petropavlovsk, as in Kiev before the war, she lived together with her two brothers, one older brother, also a professor at Kiev University, in the Faculty of Engineering, and one younger brother who ran the household. None of them had ever married. They came from an aristocratic and very religious Jewish family. Although they held high professional positions, they had remained strictly observant. They certainly couldn't find religious partners on their intellectual level; there weren't any religious young people in Soviet Russia anymore. And because of the Iron Curtain, emigration was out of the question. Not wanting to compromise their religious convictions, their only choice was to remain single. As the two older siblings were busy with their professional work, the youngest decided not to pursue a career and devoted himself to running a kosher home for them.

It wasn't easy. To find kosher food required time, energy and caution. In those years, it was considered counterrevolutionary to show any interest in religious observance, so the utmost care had to be taken not to provoke suspicion. The younger brother did all the cooking because they didn't want to rely on a non-Jewish cook, and he also did all the other household chores himself to keep their lifestyle private.

At work, Dr. Siegal manipulated things to avoid violating *Shabbos*, except in cases of *pikuach nefesh*. After hearing all this, the *chessed* she did in caring for my mother became less mysterious to me.

Her older brother was employed as an engineer in an ammunition factory in Petropavlovsk, which had been evacuated from European Russia. The most unbelievable thing was that he openly, with the permission of the K.G.B., abstained from work on *Shabbos*. This fact puzzled many, but evidently he was indispensable, and the need for ammunition was urgent.

Soon after she recovered from this illness, my mother fell ill again. Once more, she had high fever, and now a deep cough.

"It's pleurisy," Dr. Siegal said. Antibiotics were unknown in Siberia, although we had heard that recently some wonder drug called penicillin had been discovered "somewhere," a euphemism for the Western world.

My mother had to spend long weeks in bed again. The little electric stove was burning around the clock, keeping water and milk warm. The only medicine was aspirin and cough syrup. My mother's cough was deep and prolonged, and it left her very weak. During the day when I had to go out, Mrs. Kagan was of tremendous help. I repaid her with long hours of knitting for her and her medical student daughter, whom I never saw; the need for doctors was so urgent that her daughter's medical school in Omsk, four hundred kilometers east of Petropavlovsk, didn't even allow for New Year's vacations.

The "short order doctors" took a crash course for four years right after high school. "In wartime, everything is different," they used to explain. "The young doctors will gain their experience by practicing." I was happy that Dr. Siegal wasn't a wartime doctor.

Among all this work and worry, the year 1945 rolled into 1946. The new Communist Poland was put on the map again, altered geographically, economically, politically and socially. It became a satellite in the Soviet constellation.

Rumors began circulating about an eventual repatriation. When? How? We didn't know. A Polish committee was organized and meetings were permitted, though they were adequately infiltrated with K.G.B. agents and informers. A few surviving partisans travelled all the way to Siberia to be reunited with their families. Privately, they told their hairraising stories. At the meetings, they were the speakers, praising the bravery of the Soviet partisans (actually dispersed military units trapped in the Polish forests) and the help they had gotten from them. Sometimes, a gala event was organized. A few songs were sung, some poetry read, and a few speeches, all tailored to the Soviets' taste, were delivered. Culture thrived. We all began to feel that a new sunrise lurked beyond the cold horizon.

Little by little, my mother recovered from the pleurisy, but she felt very weak. Dr. Siegal advised her to stay indoors. This coincided, however, with an unexpected announcement from the K.G.B. that all Polish residents, in alphabetical order, had to come register at their headquarters. There had been similar counts during the previous years, but we were almost sure that this time it had another purpose.

When our turn came, I had to have two witnesses and the doctor's note to be able to sign for my mother. For two months after the registration nothing happened. The uncertainty was very depressing.

Meanwhile, *Purim* approached and for the first time in

Siberia we baked *hamantashen*. The filling was grated carrot mixed with dried apricot. One of our friends had discovered friends in Tashkent, also exiles, and a parcel exchange began between them. Tashkent, in Central Asia, two thousand kilometers southeast of Petropavlovsk, had a subtropical climate where grapes, apricots and peaches grew in abundance. Our friends used to sell the dried fruit by the cup.

At the same time, a group of Jews in Petropavlovsk got together a few days before *Purim*, and a decision was made to bake *matzos* on a larger scale. For this purpose, they were able to rent an apartment with a kitchen for a few days from an elderly woman who went to stay with a friend.

Every participant had to help clean and *kasher* the house. There were two exceptions, both Soviet Jews. Ravtzov, though he did not keep kosher himself, wanted *matzos* for his mother. He provided the wood. The second was Dr. Kupitzki, who was extremely happy to have *matzos* for the first time in thirty years. I offered to bake *matzos* for Dr. Siegal, but she said they had baked for themselves all these years and would do the same now.

The operation began before sunrise the day after *Purim*. Everyone brought his own flour. We brought all the *kashered* utensils, and a real *mashgiach* took care of the *kashrus*. He was Rabbi Levi Belitzki, later a very respected rabbi in New York. About twenty-five people worked, alternating functions, until late into the night. We baked over two hundred kilograms of *matzos* that day. The K.G.B. discovered the crime the day after. Informers were everywhere. They let us keep the *matzos*, but the poor woman in whose apartment this terrible outrage took place had to go to prison for two months.

When I returned home with my bundle of *matzos*, far past midnight and exhausted enough to faint, I found the light burning in our room and Mrs. Kagan near my mother's bed. My mother had high fever again, and the yellow color had returned. When Dr. Siegal saw her the next day, the expression on her face told me how serious her condition was. Dr. Siegal again began coming twice a week.

"It is more serious this time, because being ill all winter has greatly lowered your mother's resistance," she told me. "She is also anemic, and I'll add some iron to the medicine."

I asked her if my mother had pain, because she never complained.

"Of course, she has pain," the doctor replied. "I have never seen a person control herself like your mother does, not even uttering a sound or a moan. Your mother is very brave."

Pesach was approaching. Word spread that in the first days of April, right after *Pesach*, transports with Polish exiles would be sent back to Poland. An unusual excitement, a mixture of happiness and pain filled the hearts of everyone. We were happy to end the Siberian hell, but what and whom would we find upon our return? We were not given personal documents. There were only lists with names. Human cargo again.

My mother's condition did not improve. She became emaciated and weak to the point of being unable to sit up in bed. Her temperature fluctuated, and her color didn't change. Dr. Siegal did the best she could.

The doctor also knew about the repatriation and was frank in advising me not to undertake the trip. She not only advised, she insisted and pleaded that I shouldn't endanger my mother's life. Despair was a mild expression for the way we all felt. Friends and compatriots from Poland came to visit, looked at my mother, looked at me and shook their heads in pity. My mother had a vague idea of what was happening, but she was too weak to react.

What could we do? Should we remain in Siberia alone, when all the Polish citizens were leaving? Without documents, without means, without friends? Dr. Siegal and Ravtzov, our only real friends who were Soviet citizens, were planning to return to their hometown of Kiev now that the war was over. The Vaad Hatzalah parcels, the mainstay of our sustenance, would also stop. To remain in Siberia, we would be forced to accept Soviet citizenship. Wouldn't it be a slow death for both of us? As long as we had been a group of Jews together, no matter how difficult the circumstances, the togetherness, the mutual help we extended to each other, the sorrows and hopes we had shared made it possible, somehow, to survive.

But if we stayed, my mother and I would be alone, with nobody in the world. Furthermore, Mrs. Kagan informed me that when her daughter graduated in May, she would need the room. I was trapped between the fear of remaining in Siberia and the danger to my mother if we travelled. I was already familiar with the conditions in a Soviet cattle car filled with thirty to forty people travelling a stretch of ten thousand kilometers.

I had the fullest confidence in Dr. Siegal, both as a doctor and as a friend, but I still wanted to hear another opinion. I told her this, and she did not object.

CHAPTER 19

■

A Thousand Splinters

I WENT TO DR. KUPITZKI FOR ADVICE. HE LIVED IN A WELL-kept house where remnants of elegance from the past were still in evidence. Pictures hung on the walls, the floors were covered with rugs, worn but clean, and there were good pieces of furniture. It seemed that his father, as a Czarist exile, had been spared the confiscation of property and belongings by the Soviets. His family consisted of his wife, two daughters and a widowed sister with a child. His wife, the sister and his older daughter had jobs, so the family was more or less comfortable. They didn't mix with other people and lived an isolated life. His younger daughter Vera married a man from Poland and later left with the other Polish exiles.

I came late in the afternoon when the whole family was at home. They thought it was a social visit, brought tea and something to eat, and knowing that with me they could feel free to talk, they started to bombard me with questions about life on the "other side," at least, as I had known it before the war.

I felt their eagerness and longing to hear, if not to experience, how people lived in the free world. I was sitting on pins and needles, but plain courtesy dictated that I answer their endless questions.

"Yes," I said, confirming the truth of some of their wildest imaginings. Compared to their experience, plain stories about bountiful grocery stores and a choice of newspapers seemed like fairy tales. "But everything I am describing happened before the war. What it will be like now is hard to predict."

Dr. Kupitzki finished his tea, put down the cup and with a wide sweep of his hand said, "In a free world, wounds will heal sooner, people will return to their normal lives. Although it is very hard for us to be hopelessly separated, we are happy that at least our younger daughter will not feel the constricting chains which keep us prisoners in our own four walls."

Finally, I brought up the problem that was pressing on my heart. He bit his lower lip, a habit I had noticed before, and then put both his hands on the table, saying with a doubtful expression on his face, "There are a few doctors in Petropavlovsk, but the only one I would recommend is a certain army colonel who just came home for a short furlough. I am absolutely convinced that he will not come to you, and it is most likely that his orderly will not even let you in to see him. But you can try. Even in Moscow you won't find a better doctor. Here is the address."

There is no stronger motivation than necessity and hope.

The next morning was a Friday, and I went to see him. The door was opened by a soldier, the colonel's orderly. To come to a Soviet colonel without a recommendation from higher places is most unusual. I saw it on the orderly's puzzled face. When I told him, suddenly bursting into tears, that I wanted to see the colonel as a doctor because my mother was in critical condition, a nervous flicker crossed his face. It showed indecision and fear.

"The colonel is here on a short vacation. He is not seeing patients."

"Please, please ask him. Maybe he'll agree to see me for only two minutes." I was still standing in the open door, the orderly looking at me, but probably envisioning instead the enraged face of the colonel when he would tell him my request. Then he turned, not closing the door, and disappeared inside the house. In a few moments, he was back.

"Come," he said. "Go into the second room on the left."

The door to the colonel's room was open, and I went straight in. He was sitting behind a desk in full uniform but without a cap, leaning back in his chair.

"*Sadityes,*" he said. "Please sit down."

No rage, no anger? From my experiences, I equated a Soviet uniform with rage and anger. Could the inside of a Soviet uniform contain a human being? It turned out that it did. He patiently listened to my story, which I interrupted only to swallow my tears.

"You may tell Dr. Siegal that I'll be at your house tomorrow afternoon at three," he said after I had finished my story. "Tell her to meet me there."

Was I hearing right? I stood up quickly, afraid he might change his mind. He put a piece of paper and a pen in front of me, and I wrote down the address. I thanked him and left.

On the way back, braving the snow and the March wind, it occurred to me suddenly that all the excitement about getting to this doctor was only for a second opinion. Was he going to perform a miracle? Would he, by just seeing my mother, put strength into her emaciated body, or bring her instant health? In my desperate, panicky state, I realized I should not turn to this or to any doctor, but to the only One who heals, the Almighty. Only Hashem could help her and only from Him could I expect a miracle.

On Fridays, I used to fire up the big tile oven in our room a few hours later so that the heat would last over *Shabbos*. The furnace was big enough to hold more pots than our small tea kettle and one-dish-meal pot. The oven had a hinged, cast iron, tightly-fitted door which kept the heat from escaping.

The days were still short, and it was after candle-lighting time when I was finally able to make the trip to Dr. Siegal with the results of my visit to the army doctor. I had never had an opportunity to be in her apartment before. She lived very far from us and always came by sled.

For a few moments, I stood mesmerized by the sight before my eyes. Cattle cars, trains, tents, barns were swept away as if by a magician's wand. It was a Friday night from years long gone! Here in Petropavlovsk, in Stalin's Russia! A brightly lit room, a big round table covered with a snowy white tablecloth, two tall, silver candlesticks with real candles, a white embroidered cloth covering what could only be *Shabbos challos*. Fine porcelain dishes and gleaming tableware. A cheerful, serene *Shabbos* atmosphere in every corner of the room, which otherwise was very modestly furnished.

Dr. Siegal was sitting at the table when I came in. A tall man was standing in one corner *davening*. A Soviet university professor, in Stalin's time, *davening* Friday night?

The younger brother, short and slim, was busy in the kitchen readying the *Shabbos* meal. I took in every detail. Somehow, it elated me. The festivity was contagious.

"I am glad the colonel agreed to come," Dr. Siegal assured me. "I'll be on time."

On the long walk back home, I had enough time to reflect on the situation facing my mother and me. It was clear that my mother wasn't in a position to make any decisions. Would I be able to carry the load of responsibility? Inside me a voice kept repeating, "Look at the Siegal family! They have risked their freedom and possibly their lives, but they've stood steadfastly by their convictions. What moral strength they possess! What faith and trust in Hashem they have! Surely, Hashem will not abandon us in our time of need." My thoughts were shooting in a thousand directions. It's my mother's life, *my mother's*! I kept repeating to myself. The closer I came to our house the more agitated I became. The calmness I had felt in the Siegal house had blown out with the cold outside and the fear in my heart.

My mother was dozing when I returned. The flame in the little *kurnik* was flickering, the room was half dark. Above the partition, a dim light from the Kagans' kitchen supplemented the illumination. My mother woke up.

"Why are you up so late?" she asked.

"No, Mama, it is not late," I told her. "You slept so you think it is the middle of the night. I'll give you something to eat."

With effort and at additional cost, I had been able to obtain white flour from which I made toast. I gave my mother the medicine, then toast and tea with milk, and then I ate. I felt very tired. When had the day started? It seemed like a month ago.

On Dr. Siegal's orders, I had to give my mother the medicine every four hours, day and night. I didn't have an alarm clock, and I wouldn't have used one anyway, as it would have awakened the Kagans. A human being probably has a built-in, subconscious mechanism which activates itself when there is an absolute need. I went to bed and fell asleep immediately. Four hours later on the dot I was up, gave my mother the medicine, helped her with her needs and went back to sleep again.

Dr. Siegal came before three. On *Shabbos*, she didn't use the sled. She walked. I don't know what pretext she used to leave the polyclinic early. The colonel came in full uniform, his shiny boots and army coat immaculate, the insignia on his cap and shoulder straps indicating his high rank. At the sight of a full-fledged colonel on his doorstep, Mr. Kagan was completely beside himself.

The Polish doctor, a young and inexperienced Jewish exile from Poland, also asked permission to be present. When they were all seated, Dr. Siegal related my mother's medical history from the first day she had seen her. From time to time, the colonel inclined his head, interrupting only to ask a question. A few times, he looked doubtfully at my mother, then when Dr. Siegal finished, he said he wanted to examine her himself. He spent a considerable amount of time checking my mother. He wasn't in a rush, and he was very polite and serious. I was surprised at his attitude and respect. Finally, he sat back, crossed his legs and, measuring his words, looked up at me.

I was standing at the foot of my mother's bed. Before he began, I knew what he was going to say. He praised Dr. Siegal for her correct treatment and expressed regret that, under the present conditions and the overcrowding in the hospitals, a patient so seriously ill as my mother wouldn't be able to benefit from full-time medical care. To undertake the long and arduous journey back to Poland in such a condition was, in his opinion, absurd and tantamount to a death sentence.

I remember his exact words. "You will not bring her to your destination alive." With this he concluded his speech, stood up, put on his coat and shook hands with everyone present. I saw him to the door, and before he stepped outside, he repeated his last words. I thanked him heartily for his kindness, and he disappeared behind the low gate.

It was the most agonizing *Pesach* I ever experienced in my life. Six years earlier, the *Pesach* my mother and I had spent in the train on the way to Siberia was torturous enough, but then my mother was well, and a glimmer of hope that we would still meet my father sustained us.

My mother heard the doctor's words. She had her eyes closed, but weakened as she was, she fully understood their meaning. She didn't cry, didn't complain and didn't speak. She was silent as always. Dr. Siegal continued her visits, and I continued to give the same medication every four hours. There was no change in my mother's condition.

A week after *Pesach*, we heard that the repatriation had begun. Someone saw a transport from another region passing Petropavlovsk. Then we heard that some of our friends from Tokushy had left and that more transports were on their way to Poland. Tokushy, as a central railway station, served many villages where exiles were still living from the day they had been brought to Siberia.

The tension was high. In Petropavlovsk, everyone was packed and waiting for the call. Then someone came with news that a transport was due to leave in a few days from

Petropavlovsk itself. In addition, thousands of people were brought from the villages around Petropavlovsk and left waiting at the station to be loaded into the cattle cars. I, too, packed our belongings. I had to pack in any case. The Kagans' daughter would be coming home in a few weeks, and we would have to move. I wanted to cry, I wanted to pray, but I couldn't concentrate. I was as hard as a rock and yet, at the same time, broken into a thousand splinters. Then the day arrived. A transport with a list of names including my mother's and mine was due to leave in a week. It was at the end of April. At least, they were giving us advance notice, not like the fifteen minutes we'd had when we had been taken from our home.

I still didn't know what to do. I was dazed, doing things in a trance. In the kitchen, I saw Mrs. Kagan mixing white dough, which was unusual.

"I'm baking white bread, and I'll make toast for you to take along," she said. "I see that you don't know how to prepare for such a long trip."

A dam was suddenly removed. My head fell on Mrs. Kagan's shoulder, and an uncontrollable stream of tears started to flow down my face and onto her apron.

"Yes, Hashem," I cried. "You will help us! My mother will survive! She will eat the toast, every crumb of it. You will help. O Almighty, You will help."

People sometimes act in an unusual manner which cannot be explained by reason or logic. There are times when *hashgachah pratis* takes over without letting us decide for ourselves one way or the other.

When we were taken in the middle of the night and thrown into wagons to be exiled to Siberia, the families left behind were filled with grief and despair for us. And we, suffering so much during the years in exile, didn't know that for reasons known only to the Almighty, we had been chosen to survive, and our families, who seemed safe, to perish.

It wasn't my decision to take my mother out of Russia; Hashem gave me courage and hope. He turned the danger of that difficult trip into a miracle of survival.

CHAPTER 20

■

The Long Journey Back

WHEN DR. SIEGAL CAME THE NEXT DAY, I TOLD HER about my decision to leave. She did not attempt to dissuade me any longer, and good soul that she was, she just said she would come again and bring a supply of medicine. If possible, she would try to get a pint of blood to give my mother a transfusion. She kept her word.

It was an unusually early and warm spring, and the snow disappeared very quickly. Two days before our departure, Dr. Siegal came in a carriage instead of a sled, together with a nurse who was carrying the stand on which to hang the glass transfusion bottle. The doctor gave me a long list of instructions, a supply of medicine and many good wishes for my mother's recovery. I have never forgotten the *chessed* she did for my mother. She was like a flower in a jungle of thorns.

There were other good people in Russia, including truly righteous gentiles. For example, the Russian military doctor. Who had forced him to come to a desolate, poor exile family and spend a few hours of his time? Then there was the chairman of the Selsoviet in Tokushy, who had walked the streets until late at night until he found someone he trusted to warn me about my imminent deportation to the Arctic gulag. And Ravtzov, the assimilated Jew who lent us a helping hand at every turn. The appreciation I feel for them and a few others will never fade from my memory.

The last two days were like a whirlwind. I had to finish the packing, find a wagon to take us to the station and prepare adequate and suitable food for the long trip, because we knew that we would receive only the bluish-black, clay-like bread. Then I had to arrange some kind of comfortable means for my mother to make the initial trip from the house to the station, which was about four kilometers away.

The blood transfusion seemed to make my mother a bit stronger. The next day, she was able to take a few steps around the room, but then she had to lie down again. The only way for my mother to ride was on a stretcher. Here Mr. Kagan, who had become as helpful as his wife, came up with an idea.

"I have an old door in my shed," he said. "I'll cut a hole in each corner for handles, you'll spread out a few blankets, and we'll put the stretcher on top of the trunk. We can put the valises and bundles in the back of the wagon."

I did as Mr. Kagan suggested. Our old iron bed, which had accompanied us on all of our wanderings in Siberia, was folded now and waiting to make the trip with us to Poland. My mother, fully dressed, lay on the stretcher made up with blankets on top of the Kagan's bed. When the man with the wagon arrived, Mr. Kagan helped him carry our things and arranged them in the wagon as planned. Before I left the house, I gave the Kagans some nice presents, which they fully deserved. Mrs. Kagan kept wiping her eyes with her apron. As the wagon began to move, Stalinska Street disappeared from my sight and my life.

I told the driver to move very slowly so the wagon wouldn't shake. It took us two hours to reach the station which was only a half-hour's ride away. I climbed down from the wagon and told the man to wait. I went to look at my mother and felt a stab in my heart. She was so pale, so thin, so quiet, like a helpless child. My stoic, brave mother! Was I doing the right thing?

"*Nu, tchevo stoish?*" the driver asked impatiently. "Why are you just standing there?"

"Wait here," I told him. "I have to find my train."

The busy Siberian station in those days after the war was an unforgettable sight. Endless columns of trains travelled in opposite directions; numerous side tracks held long trains, some full and some empty. People were pushing, children crying. It was a tumultuous, chaotic nightmare.

The only thing I knew was the number of our train. The military guides—not guards with rifles, but still K.G.B. men—carried lists with the names and the assignments to train cars. They divided the people into groups of thirty to thirty-five in a regular car and sixty in a double car, which they called a *Pulmanovski*. No one knew who his fellow travellers would be.

Because of the slow progress of the wagon carrying my mother, the majority of passengers were already in the cars when we arrived. I was lucky to find our train without too much difficulty. Among the churning mass of people, I noticed my friend Dora Kaplinska, whom I had known before the war and met again on my apartment-seeking trip with the Polish women from the *kolkhoz* Sergeyevka. Like us, she had ended up in Petropavlovsk. I pushed my way to her, and it turned out that we were in the same car. She told me that a few other families with whom we had been close in Petropavlovsk were also in the same car with us.

I elbowed my way back to my mother. The driver had to make a big circle to bring his wagon closer to the train, which was on a side track. Ours was a regular car. There were thirty people including two children. The sight inside the car was familiar. There were two double bunks on each side of the door, with the bundles stuffed under the lower bunk. The car was high, and a wooden box was placed in front of the door instead of a ladder. I first carried my mother up onto the train, as I would a small child. Then, with the help of others, I carried up the trunk and the rest of our possessions.

If I had found a place on the lower bunk, it would have been much easier, but the lower bunks were all taken. My mother was too weak to climb up to the higher bunk, but I had no choice. One upper bunk was filled, and on the other, there was an empty space next to one wall. The first thing I did was spread a blanket and pillow so that my mother could lie down. I had to lift her up, seat her, then climb up myself to help her to her place. I put another pillow for myself next to my mother's and took out a warm quilt, because the car was drafty and it was still cold. Our little blue pail was filled with milk, and when we were more or less settled, I gave my mother the medicine and a piece of Mrs. Kagan's toast with milk. Only then did I eat a hard-boiled egg with bread.

Each car was given a list with the names of the people assigned to it. However, in the hustle of bringing our things into the car and arranging them, I had not checked the list, and I didn't know who our neighbors were to be. Worry and exhaustion overwhelmed me, and I lay down next to my mother for a while to rest. I must have dozed off when a booming bellow made me sit up abruptly.

"I don't want you on *our* bunk," a rough voice was saying. "I don't want my wife and daughters next to your sick mother. Take your *shmattes* and get out this minute!"

My tormentor wasn't a K.G.B. man but a Jew from Poland, whom everyone in Petropavlovsk knew and heard. In Petropavlovsk, he had lived on a grand scale, financed by activities that are better left untold. He, his wife, his two daughters and sons-in-law had never worked. They paraded around in black leather coats and shiny boots, the ultimate in Soviet high style, and always looked very well-fed. People appeased him, smiled at him, greeted him—and avoided him like the black plague.

I started to cry and plead with him that my mother's illness was not contagious, that she was only very weak and that, besides, her place was next to the wall and I would be between her and his family. But how dare I contradict him? In his rage, he grabbed our valises, the bundles and the trunk. With the help of his two sons-in-law, in five minutes all our belongings were on the platform in front of the car. My friends, my good close friends, lowered their heads and averted their eyes in shame and fear. No one uttered a word. I think only Aaron David and his family would have had the courage to protest, but they had left with another transport two weeks earlier. I understood my friends' positions. We were still in Siberia, still in the hands of the K.G.B.

I carried my mother outside, took down the blankets and pillows and made room for her to lie more or less comfortably on top of the pile.

The burning urgency of the moment dulled the pain, insult, hurt and anger. Only one thought occupied my mind, that I had to find a place in one of the other cars. From our other Siberian experiences with such train columns, we knew that one could never know when the train was scheduled to leave. It could be in ten minutes, an hour or two days. I took a look at the train. Our car was closer to the left end. I started with the next car to the left.

"No, we are already full," was the answer I received. The same reply was heard in the second car and the third, and every other one until the end.

I ran back, stopped for a moment and asked my mother if she was comfortable.

"Yes," she said. Only the one word.

"Don't worry, Mama. I'll find a place."

"Yes," she said again.

The train was long. In some cars, I saw people from Petropavlovsk whom I knew, some from villages and townlets in the surrounding area.

"I have a sick mother," I pleaded. "She is not contagious."

"We have no room to move as it is," was the only answer I heard. I ran from car to car. The sun was already setting. The nagging fear that the train would start moving any minute pierced my heart like a sharp knife. I started to run frantically back and forth, accomplishing nothing.

Are people without feelings? I wondered. I knew them, they knew me, so why the indifference? I found no concern, no understanding, no pity.

I ran further, then stopped for a moment to catch my breath. I looked up. Mrs. Ohr was sitting on a wooden box near the door of a train car. She was from a town not far from Lida. She was alone in Siberia. Her husband was in prison, and her only son, an officer in the Polish army, had survived the war and was waiting for her in Warsaw. I had met her many times in Petropavlovsk. She played the role of a *grande dame*, always manicured and coiffured and very selective in choosing her company. When I came closer to the car, I noticed that it was a double wagon, a *Pulmanovski*. The space between the bunks was more than twice that of the regular cars. Because of its size, it didn't seem to be too crowded in this car, but when I asked her if there was room for my sick mother and me, she gave the same answer as all the others had given. She knew my mother and knew about her illness.

By now, my will to argue was atrophied, and automatically, I started to move on.

Suddenly, I heard a voice from the depths of the car. "What? A sick woman? Mishka, let's go help."

A young man, wiry and agile, sprang down from the upper bunk, followed by a short, stocky fellow.

"Where is the sick woman?" he said. "Is it your mother? My friend Mishka and I will bring her here. There is enough room."

Mrs. Ohr, too thick-skinned to show embarrassment, no longer protested.

It was completely dark outside when the young men finished bringing in my mother on the stretcher and then our bundles. Someone lit the kerosene lantern, and I noticed that Mrs. Ohr was the only one there from Petropavlovsk.

Volodia, the quick and energetic young man who had offered to help us, took command immediately. He spoke as quickly as he acted.

"First, we'll make a place for the sick woman, and for you because you have to be near your mother. Here," he said, pointing to the far wall between the bunks, "we'll put the

205

trunk, and in front of it the bed for your mother. Hey, you," he called out to someone on the lower bunk. "You'll have to move your box under your bunk. We need the space here."

Soon, the trunk was in place and the bed unfolded. Inspired by his energy, I quickly put my mother's quilt and pillow on the bed and helped her lie down. She was drained beyond her last bit of strength. I didn't feel much better.

"Your mother needs some privacy," Volodia observed. "Do you have any sheets?"

I pulled some sheets from one of our bundles and handed them to Volodia.

"Yadzia," Volodia called in Polish in the direction of the upper bunk, from where he had jumped down before. "Look in the corner under the basket. There are some cords. Throw them to me."

In the yellowish light of the lantern, I saw a blond, young woman leaning over the edge of the bunk with a ball of string in her hand. She dropped it on the floor. In her other arm she held an infant who, disturbed from his sleep, started to cry.

"It's my wife and baby," Volodia explained, and he started to fasten the sheets together.

He moved like lightning. All I heard was, "Mishka, the hammer. Mishka, a nail. Mishka, pull the other end. Mishka, move this away." And Mishka obeyed his commander's orders like a soldier on a drill. In no time, a small area was cordoned off in the middle of the wagon.

Was this all real? I wondered. How had we gotten from the bleakest tragedy to a miracle? But then again, how would a miracle be obvious if it were not preceded by a cataclysm?

From the beginning of the war, my mother and I had overcome many challenges and tragedies, but this particular day probably left the strongest imprint on my mind. From time to time, until this very day, I have dreams in many variations, but all of the same substance—running after a departing train with luggage spread all around.

What I didn't realize at the time was that the miracle wasn't just in finding a place, but in every minute of the ensuing thirty-day trip. Had we not been forcibly removed from the car to which we had been assigned, the doctor's warning would almost surely have come to pass. In retrospect, it was clear that the Almighty had chosen for that scoundrel to act in such an inhuman manner so that we would be forced to move and my mother would survive.

Who can understand the paths along which the Almighty leads us? What may seem disastrous to us may turn out to be our salvation. Who can measure the extent of the *chessed* done to my mother and me by Volodia? I had never met him before, and motivated by sheer human compassion, he saved our lives by providing for us in the train. From the first moment we settled in the wagon, he assumed the role of a devoted son.

While we stayed on the side track for the first few days and also later, when we were already on the way, women from the nearby villages came to the station to sell eggs, baked potatoes, carrots and milk. The milk was in half-liter vodka bottles, the only product supplied in abundance. Instantly, a crowd gathered around the women, hands grabbing the most desired item—the milk bottles. Volodia, being quick as a squirrel, usually managed to get two bottles, provoking the anger of the throng.

"Why are you screaming?" he would shout back. "One is for my baby and one is for the sick woman. We have a very sick woman in our car. You can eat anything else, but she can't." If there was only one bottle, he always insisted on sharing it.

During the trip, when the train would stop at bigger stations, he and Mishka would jump off first and run to explore if there was anything edible available in the station buffet. Most of the time, all anyone could get was *kipiatok*, boiling water. But he never returned empty-handed. There were always women selling something of value—for an exorbitant price, of course.

For some reason, the medicine Dr. Siegal had prescribed for my mother had to be taken with warm milk. Every morning at five o'clock, Volodia started the little, round, iron oven whose chimney protruded through the train roof, by blowing on the kindling until the coal inside caught fire. On *Shabbos*, he insisted on warming the milk himself, disregarding my arguments that allowing a Jew to do prohibited work was like doing it myself.

"You are observant, while I am a lost soul anyway," he explained. "I wasn't Volodia before the war. I was Velvel Winterfeld from Stanislov in Galicia. My father was a pious Jew with a long beard and a long coat. I attended a *yeshivah* and wore sidelocks.

"The war changed all that. When I ran from the Germans to the Russian side, I was caught by the Soviets and sent to prison. Released after two years, sick and weak and all alone, I wandered from place to place until, reaching a village in the Petropavlovsk region, I couldn't walk anymore. I fell unconscious in the street.

"When I woke up, I was lying on the bunk near the oven in a peasant's kitchen. They turned out to be a Polish family who had lived in Siberia since the time of the Czar's rule, but they still spoke Polish among themselves. The peasant had picked me up in the street and brought me into his house. They told me later that I had been delirious and in my unconscious state spoke Yiddish. It didn't matter to them, they said. A human being is a human being. They are righteous gentiles. They nursed me back to health. I received special attention and care from their youngest daughter Yadzia, who is now my wife.

"This is what became of Velvel Winterfeld. They are good people. I am the bad one. There is no way back now. I lost my *Olam Haba*. Let me, at least, do something good here."

Tears were in his eyes and in those of all who heard him. Mine ran freely. Even Mrs. Ohr became much softer and friendlier after that.

How tragic! However, I know that after a span of over four decades he stands out in my memory as a very selfless, benevolent and helpful person. He never wanted to accept the smallest favor in return. Only once did he take a few candies for his baby, which I bought from a soldier during a stop.

Of course, it was the Almighty's will to grant my mother more years to live and spare me insurmountable, unbearable hardship, but Volodia was chosen to be the *shaliach*.

CHAPTER 21

■

Return to a Ruined World

W E RETURNED VIA THE SAME ROUTE WE HAD TAKEN
six years earlier, only more slowly. Trains carrying demobilized Soviet soldiers, German prisoners of war and endless numbers of canvas-covered platforms
with ammunition and looted goods were going from West to
East. What the bombs and war hadn't destroyed became prey
for Stalin's hordes.

The Siberian landscape, the faded, gloomy stations and
towns we passed, seemed to be even more neglected and
desolate than before. But they were still there. They hadn't
been touched by the German bombs. The Asian parts of
Russia had been spared the ravages of war.

Often, our train had to be taken to a side track to ease the
congestion. At one station, our train stopped opposite a

trainload of German prisoners-of-war. The tracks were so close that it was easy to see the uniforms and faces. Surprisingly, the prisoners in the train opposite ours looked clean, shaven and not at all underfed. Their windows didn't even have bars. The only apparent difference between our train and theirs was that our door could be opened at will and the prisoners' wagons were locked, with a guard for each car. Obviously, the prisoners were of a higher rank, not ordinary soldiers.

Although it was entirely pointless, I couldn't pass up the opportunity to express, though in the smallest way, my hatred for the Germans.

"You, from the superior race, are going to Siberia to *end* your life," I said through the window in German to one of the prisoners. "I, a *Judin*, am going back to the free world to *start* a new life."

He looked at me, squinted, pressed his lips tightly together, but didn't utter a word.

"How many Jews did you kill, you beast?" I asked.

This was too much for him to endure from a Jew. He turned away from the window.

My first encounter with German prisoners had been a few months earlier in Petropavlovsk. We had been very eager for news, still hoping for word of the repatriation, so any news was of interest. One windy, cold February morning, someone had seen three German war prisoners being held under strict security at the Petropavlovsk railroad station. This happened shortly after all their atrocities had become known. The word German was enough to conjure up a picture of a horrible monster from another planet. A few friends and I had walked the four kilometers to the station to see if they still looked like human beings, or like some wild animals from the jungle.

We found the German prisoners in the station waiting room. One corner was cordoned off with a chain, and the three captives were standing there under armed guard. They wore military uniforms, buttons missing, shoulder straps hanging loose, heads shaven. For a moment, we stood motionless, looking at them. Then, driven by some uncontrollable force, I ran forward, and before the guard could stop me, I spat right into the face of the nearest prisoner. It landed in the middle of his cheek. He wiped it off with his sleeve. My friends told me I shouldn't have done it, but if the guard hadn't motioned me away, I would have done the same to the other two.

I knew it was uncivilized and childish. Can a drop of spit avenge the loss of six million innocent lives, a million children, centuries of accumulated spiritual and cultural wealth? But at that moment, it was the only means I had to express the burning pain, rage and contempt I felt for a member of the cursed, degenerate nation which believed in *Deutchland Uber Alles*, whether he was guilty or not. No, I didn't regret my behavior.

As we continued our long journey, I was struck by a disturbing observation. Throughout the six years of living under various conditions in Siberia, our close-knit group often used the rationed water to keep our clothing and ourselves clean to avoid getting lice, the main carriers of typhus. Now, on the way back to civilization, I noticed that some of the people in the car had started twitching their shoulders and scratching their backs. There was one peasant woman on the other side of the car who was scratching more actively than the others; that was obviously where it had originated. Sixty people in one car for a month without changing clothes were an easy target for those little parasites.

The next time the train stopped, someone notified the guard. In no time, he appeared with a bagful of little white packets containing DDT. We were told to dust our bedding and clothing with the white powder, but to be careful not to let it touch the food. A day later, there was an announcement that when we would reach the next town the whole transport would be taken to the *bania*, the communal Siberian bath house.

The first time I had encountered a *bania* was in Sergeyevka. They were in use in Tokushy and Petropavlovsk as well, and by the time I came to live in those towns I was able to endure the *banias* when I had to, but my first reaction was to view them as torture chambers. Sergeyevka, which had one hundred families besides the exiles, had two *banias*. Each was a small structure, about six and a half feet by thirteen feet, not more than six and a half feet high, with an entrance foyer in front, which also served as a small nook for the clothing. It had a slanted, wooden floor with a hole at one end. In one corner was a pile of stones with a hollow space where wood was burned, thus heating the stones. Nearby stood two barrels with water. When the stones were white hot, they were thrown into the barrels. Instantly, the place was filled with a cloud of steam, making it impossible to see two inches away. The heat was suffocating, a real inferno. It was pointless to dry oneself after the bath because of the dense steam. Even the piles of clothing in the nook were drenched. Those who lived nearby were lucky, but to walk a fifth of a mile in forty to fifty degrees below zero weather after being broiled in the *bania* was a real Siberian experience.

When we reached the station with the promised *bania*, the activity started early in the morning as soon as our train was taken to a side track. In groups of about forty or fifty, we were led to town in shifts until the whole train was clean and deloused. They wanted to deliver us back to the West in a proper and civilized manner.

One morning, when our train stopped at a station, three new passengers joined our wagon, a father with two teenage girls. They didn't have any luggage, their faces were ash gray, and their eyes were swollen and red. As we later learned, they had buried the mother of the family the day before. They had come from another region in Kazakhstan and had been waiting all night on the station platform for another train carrying former exiles. Everyone in our wagon was deeply moved by their tragedy. We all offered to help in any way we could. Now, too, Volodia took command.

We noticed that all three had tears in their clothing, the traditional *kriyah* made when burying a close relative. They sat *shivah* in the car. They told us that friends from their village in Siberia who were heading for Lodz in Poland would take care of their belongings. They would have to look for them later. But no one had the heart to probe them for any other details about their tragedy, and they didn't offer any. They were too heartbroken to talk.

We passed the Ural Mountains and moved closer to the area affected by the war. The ice curtain, which had imprisoned us in Siberia for six years, had finally parted, and now, a picture of horror and destruction unfolded before our eyes. Ruins everywhere, entire forests burned down, with young, fragile saplings, here and there, clinging to the charred remnants of the mother tree. Looking from the speeding train, we sometimes saw in the distance forests of blackened chimneys, fragments of buildings with no sign of life. Many station buildings were burned or ruined by bombs, and makeshift, temporary structures were erected to receive or dispatch the endless numbers of trains. No peasant women were seen here offering milk, eggs or vegetables. If somewhere a house remained intact on the outside, the black holes that once held windows were witness to what remained inside. It was a sad sight, a sad feeling.

It reminded me of a time when, as a schoolgirl, a picture in my ancient history book of Pompeii ruined by the eruption of the volcano Mount Vesuvius made me sad for days, but it was still a detached feeling. My feeling now was intense. The closer we came to the old Polish border, the fuller the destruction and the deeper the depressing feeling.

But there were also happy moments during the trip. From somewhere, someone heard that President Truman had intervened with the British and secured one hundred thousand certificates to enter Palestine. Like lightning, the news spread from car to car. People started to sing and cry from joy, to embrace and kiss each other. About one hundred thousand Jews were returning from Russia to Poland, and everyone believed he would get a certificate. Upon arriving in Poland, however, it turned out that only a very limited number of entrance certificates had been issued to the displaced persons in the refugee camps. Many thousands of Jews, survivors of the gas chambers or Russian prisons, who tried to enter Palestine illegally were turned back to sea by the British.

One encouraging development wiped out the gloom and wretched sights we saw on the way. With the Almighty's help, my mother's condition started to improve, to the point that when we changed trains in Brest-Litovsk (Brisk), the new border town between Soviet Russia and the shrunken Poland, my mother was able to walk by herself and endure the search and registration by the Polish U.B. (the equivalent of the Soviet K.G.B.). We were now on native soil.

In Brest-Litovsk, we were given the option of choosing, as our further destination, between Lodz and Schechin, a German town not far from Berlin. This town had been given to Poland at the peace treaty in Potsdam, together with Danzig, the town of Breslau and a part of Lower Silesia, as compensation for southern and eastern Poland being annexed by the Soviets.

My mother and I joined those who went to Schechin. There were rumors that from Schechin it would be easy to cross the German border and reach the D.P. (displaced persons) camps in Munich. We said good-bye to Volodia, who went to Lodz. I bless him until this very day, wherever he is. And so we returned to a ruined world and a new start.

EPILOGUE

In the final section of the unabridged edition, the author joins the flood of refugees who gather in Germany to await transport to new lands and new lives. She meets her husband-to-be, who was, at the time, serving as Rabbi of Katowice with integrity and distinction, and together, they eventually settle and raise a family in the United States.